RONALD T. PARSONS

BEEN THERE DONE THAT

GROWING UP IN SYDNEY AND THE BUSH
1935 - 1956

National Library of Australia Cataloguing-in-Publication entry

Author:	Parsons, Ronald T., 1935-
Title:	Been there done that : growing up in Sydney and the bush 1935-1956 / Ronald T. Parsons.
ISBN:	9781921555336 (pbk.)
Subjects:	Parsons, Ronald T., 1935---Childhood and youth. New South Wales--Biography.
Dewey Number:	920.71

Cover design: Front cover illustration and back cover photo provided by the author. The cover was designed by Watson Ferguson & Company, Brisbane.

Disclaimer: Every effort has been made to ensure that the content of this book is factual. The author and publisher take no reponsibility for any errors or omissions.

Published by Boolarong Press, Salisbury, Brisbane, Australia.

Printed and bound by Watson Ferguson & Company, Salisbury, Brisbane, Australia.

In Memory of Mum, Dad and Bob.

Contents

AUTHOR'S NOTE

Before decimal currency was introduced in Australia on 14 February 1966 we had pounds (£), shillings (s) and pence (d), from having been part of the British Empire. Twelve pence or pennies made one shilling and twenty shillings made one pound. With the new system one dollar equalled ten shillings, or to put it another way, one pound equalled two dollars. Prices and values are quoted here in the currency of the day.

PROLOGUE

Until recently I considered autobiographies and memoirs written by people who'd not achieved anything remarkable in their lifetime to be ego trips. However, as the transplant patient said, 'I've had a change of heart'. I can now see value in an individual's story if written from an historical, cultural, or impressionistic point of view, as well as being a personal account.

Such a story may then be of interest to researchers, history buffs and others in addition to relatives, descendants and friends. It may even be read for amusement or as a diversion. With that in mind here's hoping you will find the ensuing words to be both enlightening and entertaining.

Ronald T. Parsons
Toowoomba, QLD.
2009

1
WHERE THE CROWS FLY BACKWARDS

'Up where the crows fly backwards to keep the dust out of their eyes.' That was the smart-alec answer to the question, 'Where do you live?' when I was a youngster growing up in Crows Nest, New South Wales.

Situated approximately three kilometres up the Pacific Highway from the northern end of the Sydney Harbour Bridge, the suburb of Crows Nest derives its name from *Crows Nest Farm Cottage* built in 1820 by Edward Wollstonecraft. A cousin of Mary Wollstonecraft Shelley who in 1818 had written the novel *Frankenstein,* he was a wealthy bachelor when he died in 1832 aged forty-nine. Edward's sister Elizabeth inherited the property and after she died in 1845 it passed to her husband Alexander Berry. On his death what was by then known as *The Crows Nest Estate* was left to his cousin Sir John Hay.

Sir John and Lady Hay took up residence in *Crows Nest House* which had been built earlier for the Berrys and after Lady Hay died in 1929 it was demolished to make way for what was popularly known as Lady Hay School, later to become North Sydney Demonstration School. Fortunately the entrance gates to *Crows Nest House* were left standing and still front the Pacific Highway today.

In the 1880's there was an urban land boom and Crows Nest had great potential for development, especially by 1893 when it became possible to either catch a train from St. Leonards, or cable tram from Crows Nest, to Milsons Point. It was then only a short ferry trip to the city. Much of the eastern side of Crows Nest was owned by Bernard Otto Holtermann who had migrated to New South Wales from Germany in 1858 when he was twenty years-old.

Shortly after he arrived in Sydney he set out for the goldfields at Hill End to join his brother. In 1868 he married Harriet Emmett in Bathurst and four years later on 19th October 1872 he struck it rich. As the major shareholder in a mining company that discovered what became known as *Holtermann's Nugget*, Bernard's fortunes changed dramatically. The firm's miners had uncovered a 290 Kg block of reef gold which was the largest known in the world at that time.

Moving to the North Shore in 1874 he built a large house with a tower that is now part of Shore Grammar School. A dedicated photographer he travelled to America two years later with an impressive photographic exhibition which included the world's largest negative. It was while in Burlington, New Jersey that Harriet gave birth on 24 July 1876 to a son whom they named after that city. Later when Holtermann's land at Crows Nest was subdivided, most of the newly-created streets were given family names. Further, because it was the custom for the rear lanes to take the same name, there is a Burlington Lane as well as Burlington Street. Other streets and lanes were named Holtermann, Ernest, Alexander, Sophia, Bernard, David, Emmett and Myrtle.

It is likely that Holtermann would have known Alexander Berry and Sir John Hay and possibly Hayberry Street is a combination of their surnames. Falcon Street is the exception as it was already in existence prior to Holtermann's subdivision.

Crows Nest Junction where Willoughby Road, Falcon Street and Shirley Road meet the Pacific Highway is the heart of Crowy, or The Nest, as some oldtimers used to call it. The hub of all the main northern routes before the Warringah Expressway opened in the early 1960's, the Junction is situated on a crest and the shops and businesses all radiate downhill. Hence the local saying, 'Going up the Crowy,' meaning walking up to the shopping centre.

In 1934 Mum and Dad married and moved into 106 Burlington Street. Located between Willoughby Road and West Street, Burlington Street is handy to both shops and public transport and is one of the most sought-after streets in the district nowadays. No doubt having one of the highest concentrations of restaurants in Sydney so close is an added attraction. However, it wasn't exactly trendy when I was growing up in 'Burlo'.

With nearly all of the one hundred and thirty or so houses in the street rented by low-paid workers and their families, most residents lived from one pay-day to the next. It was especially hard during the Depression, the War years and the years immediately following.

The fact that there were rent restrictions during those years resulted in landlords spending as little as possible on their rental properties. Consequently, the majority of the houses on the eastern side were rundown. By contrast, Wollstonecraft on the western side of Crows Nest was fairly affluent. Indeed, in the late 1940's I used to deliver newspapers before school and on weekends to that area and Sir Earle Page, an ex-Prime Minister of Australia, lived on my paper route.

As far as I know all of the people in our street were Australian – born of English, Scottish, Welsh or Irish ancestry. Otherwise they had come from those countries. There were other nationalities in the district. Some of the shopkeepers in Crows Nest were southern European and we bought our fish and chips from 'Old Joe', a Chinese whose shop was in Willoughby Road. A census taken two years before I was born in 1935 showed that in the North Sydney area 55% of the population were Church of England (Anglican), 20% were other Protestant and 20% were Catholic. I was never aware of any animosity between Protestants and Catholics but perhaps I was naive. The population of Australia was 6,629,839.

106 is one of a single-storey terrace of four. It had four rooms and what was called the lavatory up the backyard. The land on which the house stands (it is still there but upgraded) measures approximately 5.5 metres x 45.5 metres. In our street there were two double-fronted sandstone cottages, half a dozen two-storey

terraces, a few single and double-fronted weatherboard homes, numerous semi-detached brick cottages, a row of single-fronted Federation houses, groups of similar terraces to ours and a corner shop with a bakery opposite where Sophia Street crosses over. At the Willoughby Road end of Burlington Street there were a few shops including a chemist, ladies hair salon and sporting goods store.

The front room of 106 was meant to be the parlour, or lounge room, but Mum and Dad made it their bedroom. Down the hall was the lounge room then the kitchen and what was called the wash-house was at the rear. I slept in a cot then on a settee in the front room with my parents until my brother Bob was born in January 1943, after which the settee and I were moved into the lounge room. When brother John was born in September 1949 he got the cot and Bob who by that time had a single bed joined me in the lounge room. We used to say Dad had the seven-year itch after fathering three sons at those intervals.

Other families, especially those with both boys and girls had more difficulty accommodating them. Opposite us one family had a daughter and five sons. Judy the daughter was fortunate to have her own bedroom whereas the boys shared one between them. I have known Russell since we were in class 1A at Lady Hay School in 1942. His family lived behind us in Ernest Street. With his parents and five sisters taking up the bedrooms, he and his older brother Gordon slept in a double bunk in the tiny pantry.

Many other playmates (not the girlie magazine ones) had to share covered-in verandahs as bedrooms and in some instances a bedroom would be divided in half with sheets of masonite and/or curtains in order to accommodate both sons and daughters. No one seemed to mind though. What you haven't had you don't miss as the old adage goes.

Before a family of four moved into the terrace two doors up from us during the war it was rented by a Salvation Army couple and their six children. It amused my parents and even me at age seven to hear them chatting while they were lined up waiting to use the backyard lavatory each morning.

The lavatories were about a third of the way up the narrow backyards and were built back-to-back with only a single wall of brick separating them. If someone was in the neighbouring one at the same time you could hear everything. The structures had a curved corrugated iron roof and the seat was a plank with a round hole. The water closet sat up above on two pipes and you pulled a chain to flush the bowl. Thankfully our street was sewered. Our lavatory as with many had a choko vine growing over it.

106 and 108 shared a dual chimney in their front rooms and there was another dual chimney serving the fuel stove in the kitchen plus the copper in the wash-house. Later on we got a gas stove in the kitchen and Dad installed a woodchip heater over the bath. Up until then we had to boil water in the wood-fuelled copper and carry it over to the bath in a bucket.

In 1947 I climbed up on the roof and took a couple of photos with my Box Brownie camera. The front two rooms had a gable roof of corrugated iron and the rear rooms had a skillion roof.

When the photos are looked at today a skyline dotted with chimneys is a notable feature of the landscape.

After rent restrictions were eased many of the houses in Crows Nest and other suburbs came up for sale in the 1950's and were purchased by the tenants if they could afford it. The properties being tenanted were less valuable than if they had been Vacant Possession. Many tenants were able to purchase their home for approximately £100 deposit and a £900 mortgage. Some tenants were offered around £300 to move out by their landlord. Dad purchased 106 in 1958 and they occupied it until Dad died in 1994 and Mum moved into a nursing home in 2003.

Once people owned their homes most started doing them up. especially as Australia became more prosperous in the 1950's and 60's. For some reason Dad never bothered to renovate 106 after he owned it. I'm sorry to admit my brothers and I were reluctant to invite friends home as we were ashamed of our place when others were done up. We nicknamed it 'The Cave'. At least Mum kept it clean and when we did bring someone home Mum's bubbly personality made up for the squalid surroundings.

2
THE DEPRESSION AND WAR YEARS

I was born on Thursday 19 September 1935 at Royal North Shore Hospital (RNSH) St. Leonards. I was very young at the time so I don't remember much about that day (OLD JOKE). Actually I don't recollect much about anything prior to 1940.

The whole of the lower North Shore was called St. Leonards in the very early days of settlement before it was divided up and renamed North Sydney, Milson's Point, etc. That is why St. Leonards railway station is between Artarmon and Wollstonecraft yet St. Leonards Park is between North Sydney and Cammeray.

One of my few pre-war memories is Friday night shopping with my parents up the Crowy and being fascinated by the neon sign on top of the Crows Nest Hotel. A little neon man appeared to climb up a ladder and paint the advertisement. The sign was removed when the war was on Sydney's doorstep in 1942.

Another memory etched in my mind happened on 14 January 1939. It was one of the hottest days recorded in Sydney and smoke from bushfires shrouded the city. Mum and I were on our way to visit her mother who at that time lived above a shop on the Pacific Highway just down from the Junction. The sky was a glowing orange colour and the sun was a crimson ball. It was like you'd imagine the end of the world.

I also remember my first day at kindergarten at Lady Hay school. We sat on rattan mats and were given coloured sticks to play with. Art has been a lifelong interest and the colours of the dyes made a lasting impression. They were similar to the beautiful colours of the Indian postage stamps and garments.

Out in the playground one day a couple of boys tried to bully me so I challenged one of them after school. Mum told Dad that when she met me at the McHatton Street gate that afternoon and asked why I was late, I said, 'I had to fight a kid'. They didn't bully me after that. Dad had been an amateur boxer and had taught me a few of the basics. A southpaw, in my late teens I trained with Jack Southern at the Bjelke Peterson gym in Castlereagh Street. I don't know if there was any connection with Joh and Flo in Queensland.

After second class the boys and girls were separated at our school. The girls went to the *Big Girls* building near the Pacific Highway and the boys to the *Big Boys* building on the western side. Beyond that was a large paddock with rows of air raid trenches.

Dad had an old Morris Cowley tourer which he was able to keep running even during the war years. He worked for the Shell

Oil Company at its Gore Bay terminal and was allocated an extra amount of petrol during the years when it was rationed, probably because he was a shift worker in an essential industry. Petrol rationing in Australia did not end until 1950. Although he was untrained he was clever with engines and anything mechanical. In later years when one of the engineers at the *Oil Works* as it was called, went on leave Dad was trusted to take over his duties. Dad also dabbled in the Shell Chemical Laboratory and made his own hair cream.

Having a car meant we could go for drives and picnics on weekends when Dad wasn't working shiftwork. Blackout regulations stipulated that motor vehicles had to have the headlights hooded and a continuous white stripe painted around the bottom part of the bodywork and mudguards. Dad made his own headlight hoods which looked like slotted top hats. Many cars had charcoal gas bags on frames over their roof to power them.

The windows of houses had to be blacked-out and a type of tarpaper was used along with criss-crossed tape stuck on the window panes to prevent flying glass. Many buildings in the city had sandbags stacked up in front and there was barbed wire strung along the ocean beaches. An air raid siren was fitted to a telegraph pole at the lower end of our street and tested every Sunday at 1.00 pm.

Occasionally fire evacuation practice was held at the two-storey bakery building on the corner of Burlington and Sophia Streets. Air raid wardens and firemen would rig up a canvas chute to an upstairs window, similar to the emergency chutes used on large aircraft today. To us kids it was a slippery dip and we volunteered to *evacuate* over and over again.

Many items that people take for granted were rationed during and after the war. Mum had a ration book which had stamps limiting the purchase of basic items such as butter, meat and so on. To supplement our diet Dad had a *Victory Garden* in the backyard and grew tomatoes, lettuce, spinach, potatoes, pumpkin, peas, beans, chokos and spring onions.

The war's influence was everywhere. If I was lucky enough to get a Dinky toy at Christmas it was a tank or army truck. Otherwise, it was a war comic though one year Dad carved me a toy yacht. He remained a civilian as he worked in an essential industry. However, his three younger brothers were in the army.

Even cartoons at the cinema were influenced by the war. For example, Walt Disney's *Donald Gets Drafted* (1942), *Private Pluto* (1942) and *Der Feuhrer's Face* (1944) which had a great song that all the kids would sing.

The pictures, or flicks, (movies) were a cheap form of entertainment for the masses and *Sat'dy Arvo* was an outing to the cinema for most kids. There were two cinemas in Crows Nest, the Sesqui on the Pacific Highway and Hoyts in Falcon Street on the site of the present-day Woolworths. The brick wall along the Alexander Street side of Woolies is part of the old cinema.

Competition was fierce between the two picture theatres for the Saturday afternoon trade and occasionally children were enticed with free gifts. Hoyts handed out steel helmets one week and gas masks another, most likely war surplus purchased in bulk. If there was a war film on some kids would wear them while watching. It was hilarious to see the younger ones sitting there wearing a full-sized steel helmet and gas mask. They looked like giant bugs.

The *Sesqui* had a birthday club and after interval Reg Quartly, a popular Sydney radio personality would stand on stage in front of the curtain, call out a birthday boy or girl's name, whereupon he or she would step up to loud applause and receive a free Gartrell White sponge cake. When all the birthday cakes had been handed out everyone would sing 'Happy Birthday' then the main feature would begin. It might interest readers to know that in those days Gartrell White Bakeries used to make their deliveries in electric-powered vans. They were silent except for a soft whirring sound.

One year there developed intense rivalry between the two cinemas for the most cartoons. The *Sesqui* would advertise four cartoons for the coming Saturday. The following week *Hoyts* would announce five and so it went on until it reached the point where there was a whole early morning session showing twenty cartoons.

Usually the afternoon session showed a newsreel, maybe a James A. Fitzpatrick travelogue, a couple of serials and cartoons plus a short western. Hopalong Cassidy was the favourite with the boys because he didn't sing or kiss girls like some of the other cowboys. After interval there might be a comedy, pirate or war picture. The films were not usually as long as they are today. Serials were a way of getting repeat business. There were ten to fifteen episodes and except for the last one, each would end with a cliff-hanger so that you had to come back the following Saturday to see the outcome. Personal favourites were 'The Phantom Empire' (part western, part sci-fi), 'The Green Archer' and 'The Spider' (both caped crusaders).

It was a custom for many families to have a roast dinner for lunch on Sundays. After I had arrived back home late for lunch several times, Dad said I must stop playing and come home to lunch as soon as I heard the one o'clock siren. If I was late again I would get the strap. Being hit on the backside and legs with a leather belt was a common form of punishment for boys back then. Dad wasn't to know that often I was playing in the bush at Spenno – the suspension bridge at Northbridge – or paddling a tin canoe in Middle Harbour. My mates and I had made the canoe out of a sheet of corrugated iron and a fruit case. Also I was a bit of a rebel and as a consequence frequently got the strap.

Some afternoons after school a few of us kids would take our trolleys, or billycarts, and go from door-to-door collecting waste paper, rag or metal for the war effort. However, mostly I enjoyed drawing and listening to children's programmes on the wireless, or radio as it is called nowadays. The ABC had the *Argonauts Club* while the commercial radio stations had serials and shows such as *Yes, What?* which was about a gullible Schoolmaster and his cheeky pupils.

Other favourites were *The Air Adventures Of Biggles*, *The Search For The Golden Boomerang* and *Dad and Dave*.

In summer there was Daylight Saving and we were able to play cricket and other games out in the street till late. There was little or no traffic as few people in Burlington Street had cars and petrol was scarce anyway. Sometimes in the school holidays Mum would take me for a bus ride to Epping or Manly. I remember going along the Epping Highway in a red and cream coloured double-decker at North Ryde and there on both sides of the road, as far as I could see, were row upon row of army trucks and jeeps destined for the war up north. If it was a hot day we would catch a tram to Balmoral Beach and have a swim.

Nearly all of our relatives lived at Crows Nest within walking distance. Nana and Pa (short for Grandpa) Parsons lived at 70 Falcon Street and their youngest daughters Kath and Coral were single and lived there also. Often on a weekend I would go around to Nana and Pa's house to play with some of my cousins. On Saturday the local SP bookie – short for starting price bookmaker – would come in the back gate to take bets on the races. There were no local TAB's and offcourse betting was illegal. Both grandmothers would have the odd shilling each-way bet to try and bolster the weekly housekeeping. There always seemed to be a lot happening at number 70. It was a double-fronted brick house with a large backyard divided by a line of beaut trees for climbing.

Sometimes Auntie Coral would invite a U.S. Serviceman to her home and more often than not they would lay down on a rug spread out on the back lawn and chat. Us kids would deliberately stare at the yank until finally he bribed us to go away. Usually we got those flat strips of chewing gum which weren't available in Australia, or some coins. One time I scored a gob hat off an American sailor.

The sound of ships' sirens and foghorns coming from Sydney Harbour could be heard in Burlington Street as could the steam trains at St. Leonards goods yards at night. However, on the night of Sunday 31 May 1942 there was the sound of explosions and gunfire. As it turned out three Japanese midget submarines had entered the harbour. The gunfire was from Australian and American warships. The 'USS Chicago' hit one sub as well as a ferry, some other ships and harbourside homes on the North Shore. The other two subs were sunk by depth charges according to the official press release. Twenty-one Australian sailors were killed when their vessel was torpedoed at Garden Island.

Eight days later the Rose Bay area was shelled by an offshore Japanese submarine. The authorities couldn't hide those two episodes but they did keep secret the fact that eighteen ships were sunk on the east coast by Japanese and German subs from 1942 to 1944. The Sydney 'Sun' newspaper revealed this some twenty years after the war.

Our neighbour in 102 was one of the few people who built a backyard air raid shelter in Burlington Street. He dug a huge hole, laid a corrugated iron water tank in it on its side and covered it with soil. The problem with trenches and shelters was that they filled with water when it rained. Some of the more well-off families in Sydney evacuated their children to the Blue Mountains after the submarine attacks. Fortunately those of our relatives and neighbours in the armed forces came through the war unscathed.

On 15 August 1945 the day it was announced World War 2, or *Dainiii Sekai Taisen* as the Japanese called it, was over, a bunch of us kids formed a makeshift band of both boys and girls, using garbage tin lids as cymbals and kerosene tins as drums. Led by Russell's brother Gordon we marched along Ernest Street and up Willoughby Road making a heck of a din. As we turned into Falcon Street past the packed Crows Nest Hotel, drinkers spilled out onto the footpath cheering us on and throwing coins which we willingly picked up. We couldn't leave the street littered, could we?

3
FAMILY TIES

Dad's grandfather Joshua Parsons was born at Preston-next-Faversham, Kent in 1851. Joshua's future wife Mary Ann Steer was christened at Marlebone All Souls Church on 20 February 1854. Her parents Henry and Eliza lived in Edgeware Road, London and I believe a brother of Mary was a champion boxer.

In 1876 Joshua and Mary paid their own passage to South Australia, arriving at Port Adelaide aboard the twelve hundred ton sailing ship *Robert Lees* on 11 January 1877. A son, Charles aged two, was with them and they brought their own furniture. A few weeks later on 7 February Mary gave birth to another son they named Thomas (Pa).

After leaving school Pa first worked as a boundary rider for Sidney Kidman before going to sea. Employed on Huddart Parker Line ships including *Ulimaroa*, *Zealandia* and *Riverina* he eventually settled in Sydney, married and had four sons – Stanley and Harold (both of whom died young) Harry and Lenny. When his wife died not long after, Pa or Sparrow as he was also known, married a second time. He met Veronica Crowe whilst he was working on a Manly ferry. Veronica – nicknamed Nell – lived at Paddington and made the ferry trip to Manly where she worked as a Nanny. Her father James Patrick Crowe was born near Kilfenore in Ireland and came to New South Wales after serving in the British Army in the Crimean War. He joined the NSW Police in 1864 and married Mary Anne Rawlings at St. James Church, Sydney on 25 January 1868. Mary's father Edward had been born in England and her mother in Ireland. Edward was a stonemason.

Thomas and Veronica had seven children, namely Ronald Thomas (Tom – my father), John James (Jack), Dorothy (Dot), William (Bill), Kathleen, Coral May, Francis (Frank) and twenty-six grandchildren, yours truly being the first-born grandchild.

Mum, whose maiden name was Mitchell, had ancestors arriving in Sydney as far back as the third fleet in 1791 on her father's side. The most notable one was John Grono, a Welshman, who arrived on 3 May 1799 as Boatswain aboard *HMS Buffalo*, together with his wife Elizabeth and two of their three children. He and his family eventually settled at Pitt Town on the Hawkesbury where he became a successful farmer and shipbuilder. He also managed the neighbouring farm owned by Governor Bligh and was master on his own and other ships. Sealing in New Zealand waters in the early 1800's he is credited with naming Milford Sound and other places in the South Island. The Gronos are buried in the grounds of Ebenezer Church which is the oldest in Australia.

William George Mitchell was born in Sydney on 4 March 1888. His future wife Violet Wales Pollock was born in 1890 on the Prince of Wales' birthday. Violet's mother Emily Quigley had been born in Bathurst but her father Adam Pollock, a blacksmith by trade, was from Glasgow, Scotland. Violet and William (Bill) married on 1 February 1911 and rented a house in Yurong Street, Darlinghurst. They had four children – William (Billy), Thelma Pearl (my Mum), Violet May (Girlie), Allan Roy and six grandchildren.

Bill Mitchell worked on the tramways and managed the tramways cricket team. He died of TB when I was only six months old, but I've been told he had a wonderful personality and was a good friend of Stiffy and Mo, the well-known comedy team. The Darlinghurst-Woolloomooloo district became a dangerous place in the 1920's with the razor gangs so Mum's father transferred to the North Sydney tramways in 1926 and rented a house in Union Street.

Later the family moved to the Tramways House in Ridge Street then Whaling Road, North Sydney. At the height of the Depression in 1931 Mum's older brother Billy who had lost his job and was unable to find work, fell into a state of depression and jumped to his death at The Gap. Near South Head it was a notorious place for suicides. Billy was only twenty years old. He and his father were buried in unmarked graves at Northern Suburbs Cemetery as the family could not afford headstones. However, years later Mum rectified that.

In 1937 Mum's mother married again. Augustine Leslie McMahon worked for the Postmaster General's Department

(PMG) as a telephone linesman. Uncle Gus as we grandchildren were told to call him had fought and was gassed on the Western Front in the so-called Great War. He enlisted in the AIF on 20 August 1915 and returned to Australia in February 1919. I have his WW1 British War Medal and Victory Medal. McMahons Point on Sydney's North Shore is named after a relative of his who had owned the land and was Mayor of the local council in the 1880's.

Gus was a happy and kindly man. He and Nana loved to sing and tell funny stories. They liked to have a good laugh as people used to say. Whenever Nan was telling a story she would act it out. I was home one day when Mum, Nana and Auntie Nora, who was married to Harry Parsons, were having their regular Tuesday get-together at 106. Nana suddenly got up and disappeared down the hall intending to act out a story. Auntie Nora who was English and of a serious disposition said to Mum, 'Where's she gone? Have I offended her?'

Sometimes Nana Parsons and some of Mum's neighbours would also come to the Tuesday lunches which continued for about forty years. Mum was friends with lots of women in our street and her happy nature earned her various nicknames. Some people called her Thelly, others called her Sem or Pip.

Thelma Pearl Mitchell and 'Tom' Parsons were married on 12 May 1934 at Christ Church, Lavender Bay by Reverend Frank Cash who is remembered for his series of photographs depicting the building of the Sydney Harbour Bridge. Mum had only turned twenty a couple of days before the wedding and as she was under the legal age of twenty-one Dad had to obtain her father's consent. Mum was a very open person and was never able to keep a secret. One day she told her father that Tom was going to ask for her hand in marriage that night. Dad guessed that she would have warned her father so he decided to have a little joke.

'You are aware Thelma and I have been going together for some years Mr. Mitchell. There is something I want to ask you,' said Dad.

'Yes Tom. What is it you want to ask?'

'Can you lend me five quid?' replied Dad.

There were no wedding photos or honeymoon. The young newlyweds couldn't afford it. They moved straight into 106. When he was single Dad used to go sailing in the eighteen-footer races. There was a crew of about nine plus the captain Bill Barnett, a boat builder. Most of the crew were there purely for ballast as they didn't have trapezes in the 1930's. Dad also used to go fishing whenever he could.

Mum assumed he would give up the sailing and fishing when they got married and spend the weekends at home or take her out. She was more the social type rather than the outdoor type and this caused a lot of rows. Dad eventually gave up sailing but he, Mum, Nana McMahon, Uncle Gus and I would watch the eighteen-footers from Manns Point at Greenwich on the weekends. Dad had sailed on *Waratah* but I favoured *Swansea.*

After the war Dad bought an old twenty-six foot launch with a cabin and two bunks. He restored and christened her *Tuna*. Twenty years later he sold *Tuna*, bought a smaller open boat, added a cabin and christened her *Mate*. He once told me he would have liked to have been a boatbuilder in Tasmania. As well as being competent with engines he had the ability to have been a great boat builder. A dinghy he built in our backyard was added proof of his shipwright skills.

Mum went out on the harbour with him for a while when he had *Tuna* but it wasn't her cup of tea. However, his brother Bill and I would go with him. We'd walk down to Gore Bay where *Tuna* was moored about ten o'clock at night, motor round to one of Dad's special fishing spots at Kirribilli or Berry's Bay and wait for the right moment. A good time was an incoming tide just on dawn. I slept on one of the bunks while we waited. When the fish were on they were really on. We'd catch a lot in a short time then head home. I loved being out on the harbour at night with a thermos flask of hot tea and some sandwiches listening to Dad and Uncle Bill yarning before I turned in.

Our earliest holidays as I recall were camping at Narrabeen Lakes with Jeannie and Ronnie who were friends and neighbours. Mum would later remind me that Ronnie who was a good drawer used to coach me of an evening until he joined the army and went to New Guinea. I used to liken people to film stars when I could and Ronnie looked a lot like Gene Autry.

Towards the end of the war we started going by steam train to Koolewong on Brisbane Water for our holidays with Nana and Gus. We rented an old weatherboard house between the railway line and road with a jetty opposite. Usually a rowing boat was included for going fishing. Some days we all hopped aboard then Dad and Gus would row us down to Woy Woy where Mum and her mother did the shopping. Dad and Uncle Gus would refresh themselves with a beer at the pub while I got a Margin's lemonade or a McNiven's ice cream and if I was lucky a comic book.

One of my jobs was to stand down the backyard near the railway line and wave to passenger trains. The idea was to get the engine driver or fireman to toss us a big lump of coal for the fuel stove, or to have an obliging passenger throw me a newspaper.

From the late 1960's on, many of the neighbours and some of our relatives moved to the Central Coast. Mum and Dad remained at 106 but purchased a weekender at Woy Woy in the early 1970's with money they inherited after my brother Bob died of cancer. He was only twenty-seven and had worked at the ABC.

At the end of the war Dad's brother Frank married Muriel (Mibs) Russell. Auntie Muriel's parents and sisters lived in a flat on the top floor of what we called 'The Temple' at the northern end of Balmoral Beach. Mr. Russell was employed by Mosman Council as the caretaker. The Temple was a multi-level concrete building the roof of which was an amphitheatre and there were secret passageways inside. It was built for the faithful to watch a messenger of God enter through Sydney Heads, walk across the water and address them. A holy man called Jiddu Krishnamurti did in fact speak from the Temple's stage in 1925. However, he arrived here by ship like most people did back then.

I was invited to stay with the Russells some weekends. The Temple was right on the beach near a rock pool with the much larger net pool further along. At the crack of dawn I'd be up swimming with the Russell twins, Rose and Marie, who were about the same age as me. We'd walk around the rocky shoreline to Chinaman's Beach and collect long shells called Chinese fingernails, sunbathe in the amphitheatre and late in the afternoon when the beachgoers had gone home I'd help rake the beach with Uncle Frank and Mr. Russell who recorded and stored any valuables found prior to delivering them to the Council's Lost Property Office on the Monday. Sometimes at dusk we'd fish off the point and occasionally Bob Dyer the radio and later TV Quizmaster would be fishing nearby. He and his wife Dolly lived at Balmoral at the time.

In my early teens on summer weekends some mates and I would catch a double-decker bus to Manly where we'd swim in the harbour pool with its slippery dips and pontoons before buying fish and chips for lunch. Afterwards we'd dive for coins off the ferry wharf. A favourite trick was to surface pretending not to have retrieved the coin then casually take it out of your mouth. After all it was entertainment.

On other days I would go with my cousin Kevin or a mate down Shirley Road to Gore Bay where Dad had his boat. To get out to *Tuna* Dad used a punt which was tied up to the Salvage Wharf. There was only one oar which he used to scull from the stern. I didn't like that system so I rigged up a jury mast and attached an old curtain I got from Mum as a sail. The oar served as a rudder. My mate and I would usually sail around the bay, or cove as it is known today, to the other side of Berry's Island where there were two hulks tied alongside each other. One was an old paddle-wheeler and the other was the decommissioned

1918 destroyer *HMAS Stuart*, one of the Scrap Iron Flotilla of Tobruk fame. However, one day we got overly adventurous and sailed down the harbour as far as the bridge. It was easy going with the strong wind behind us but without a fin keel we couldn't sail back, so we had to scull. Never again!

May 24 was Empire Day or Cracker Night as we preferred to think of it. Neighbours would build a bonfire in Burlington Lane and everyone would stand around it to keep warm and let off their fireworks. Skyrockets, Catherine Wheels, Volcanoes and Double Bangers were too expensive for me so I'd spend the money my parents gave me for crackers on Tom Thumbs. To get my money's worth I'd separate the forty per string and light them individually from a piece of burning rope. That way the tiny crackers and slow-burning rope lasted while I watched the neighbours' fireworks go off.

One little money-making business I had was reproducing toy cars. First I'd mix some Plaster of Paris with water in a tobacco tin and press a toy racing car upside-down into it to make a mould. Then I would melt some sheet lead torn from the roof of the nearby disused bakery stable over a flame and ladle it into the mould. When it cooled I painted a number on both sides and Bob's your uncle. It was ready to sell or be traded to classmates. Lots of toys were made of lead back then.

In winter I often went camping with Kevin who lived opposite 106 and Terry from Ernest Street. On Friday afternoon we would catch a train from St. Leonards to Pymble, then go by private bus to St. Ives and hike down to Bungaroo Valley. We had a small tent but usually camped under a rock ledge that had a hole in it which served as a chimney for our fire. After we had our evening meal we yarned, drank billy tea and smoked roll-your-own cigarettes like Chips Rafferty the Australian film actor. On Saturday and Sunday we would trek up to the Trig station or swim in the rock pool near our camp and catch yabbies to cook. I had an old stockwhip with a shoelace tied to the end to make a good cracking sound. To catch a yabby I tied the shoelace around a piece of bread and lowered it into the rock pool. The water was so clear you could see right to the bottom. One day I watched as a yabby emerged from between some rocks and when it clutched the bread I was so excited I flicked too hard. We searched and searched until eventually we found the yabby up in the fork of a tree. Sunday afternoon we packed up and travelled home ready for another week at school.

4
ALRIGHT PLEASE

Having breezed through primary school I got a bit of a shock starting high school. At Lady Hay School I was always up around the top of the A classes. I played the fife in the fife and drum band and won various art poster competitions as well as getting top marks for essays and maths.

It was believed to be the rule that the top students went on to North Sydney Boys High in Falcon Street. However, I was sent to North Sydney Technical High School (NSTHS) in Blue Street opposite North Sydney Railway Station. Falcon Street would have suited me fine as it was only a five minute walk from 106. What I didn't know until years later was that during the war NSTHS had been upgraded and that the NSW Department of Education had asked the principals of Northern District feeder schools to encourage the best students – with parental concurrence – to go to NSTHS to build and be part of its quality and status. All Mum and Dad were told was that 'Your son has been selected for advanced education at North Sydney Technical High School'.

The school had its beginnings in 1878 when it had connections with the Church of Scotland. Up until it was closed in 1969, and the site destined to become Greenwood Plaza, it went through numerous changes. Today's Greenwood Plaza owes its name to the first headmaster, Nimrod Greenwood, and the original sandstone building along with the extension is now a popular bar and restaurant. Although NSTHS no longer exists there is an exceptionally active old boys union. The Old Lions take their name and colours (black and gold) from the school's emblem and have their own room appropriately named *The Lions Den* in the old sandstone building for which they fought long and hard in the 1980's to save from being demolished. The school motto was *Carpe Diem* which translates to *Seize The Day*. Thanks to a couple of movies that motto is fairly well known. 'Make the most of today' is good advice.

Our most recognisable Old Lion would probably be Dick Smith who I believe was inspired when he read a biography of MacPherson Robertson. 'MacRobertson', the *Old Gold* and *Freddo Frog* chocolate king was also an aviation enthusiast, Antarctic expedition backer and philanthropist. One high school classmate whom I later worked alongside for a time at Channel 7 in Epping is Ken Shadie. Ken went on to become a freelance writer and wrote scripts for *The Mavis Bramston Show*, *Number 96*, *The Paul Hogan TV Specials* and the first *Crocodile Dundee* movie – the TV Specials and movie in conjunction with Hoges. Another classmate who was interested in the technical side of movies from an early age also worked at Channel 7.

Because of the high calibre of students I only managed B classes at NSTHS and one year I was in a C class. I'd like to think it was because I mucked about and played the clown. At about age fourteen I began a difficult adolescence becoming gawky, pimply and so on. In order to deflect the spiteful comments I became a joker. I also lost myself drawing comics which I circulated in class.

Shortly after I started at NSTHS in 1948 a rostrum with a large replica of the school badge mounted on a pole was erected near the Tuck Shop where assembly was held. Our Headmaster at the time – J. B. Ireland – would speak first and always preface his speech with the words 'Alright Please' which was his way of telling us to settle down and be quiet. Don't get me wrong, JB was a well-liked principal, but the point is whenever he spoke those two words he tended to spit. This led to comments such as, 'You can spray that again'.

In 1949 the school published a school magazine entitled *The Lion* so I introduced an unofficial class magazine called 'Alright Please'. As well as the name on the masthead there was a cartoon illustration of J.B. on the rostrum prefacing his speech and the assembled students protecting themselves with umbrellas.

On Saturday 17 September of that same year Mum gave birth to her third son. Earlier when Mum and Dad were wondering what to call the baby if it was a boy they asked me what I thought.

Being the clown for some reason I suggested 'Moses'. Mum got her own back on me though.

The Monday following the birth of my baby brother I was summoned to the Headmaster's office. Wondering if it was about my 'Alright Please' magazine I was greatly relieved when JB said there was a telegram for me stating 'Mum and Moses both well'. JB then asked me, 'Who is Moses'? Mum and Dad had chosen 'John William' incidentally.

Also about that time our English teacher Mr. Carew asked the class to write an essay on any topic. Mr. Carew who was also responsible for the school magazine told us the best one would be published in the next edition of *The Lion*. Having a vivid imagination I wrote a humorous story about spies, an eccentric inventor, his beautiful daughter and her boyfriend. Although it wasn't chosen for the magazine Mr. Carew asked me to lengthen the storyline and turn it into a script for the annual playday. This I did and with extra gags suggested by the actors it was a hit on the day. I played the role of the *Inferior Decorator* painting the room in which the play was set. Sometimes the annual playday was held at the Independent Theatre in Miller Street and at other times at the North Sydney Anzac Memorial Club.

NSTHS had a prestigious boys choir with two hundred and fifty voices. Our music teacher Mr. R.C. (Banjo) Paterson had us performing at the Sydney Town Hall and making recordings. I was a soprano in first year but was put in the alto section when my voice was breaking the following year. Banjo was popular with the boys and was even able to instil a love of classical music in us. I remember one day he jotted down a list of composers on the blackboard – Debussy, Offenbach, Sibelius, etc., etc., which caused much whispering and laughter. When he asked to be enlightened as to the cause of all the jocularity he was told by one of the boys, 'De pussy often barks'.

There was a lot of fun in second year. It had taken a while to get used to the high school culture in first year and from third year on we had to knuckle down for the Intermediate and Leaving Certificate exams. One of the shocks on starting high school was the unofficial initiation ceremonies. I got off comparatively lightly having my head held in a toilet bowl while it was flushed repeatedly. I also acquired the nickname *Parsnips* which was soon shortened to *Snips.*

Some of the pranks played in second year were like something out of a slapstick comedy. Our metalwork and woodwork classes were held in two weatherboard classrooms, or 'dogboxes' as we called them. One of the woodwork teachers was a real crank and had a habit of kicking the door open when he was about to enter. Thinking we'd teach him a lesson we loosened the screws of the door hinges one day and made ourselves look busy when he approached. Sure enough he put his foot to the door and as it crashed to the floor we had to force ourselves to look surprised. I don't know if he was awake up to us but it cured him for a while. He just muttered, 'Somebody put that door back up', and carried on as usual.

An item from our class 2B notes in that 1949 issue of *The Lion* reads as follows:-

> 'The funniest incident that took place this year was when the leg of the blackboard broke and fell on Mr. ———. Marshall was sent out of the room as it was thought by the teacher that the leg had been purposely sawn and he was there to push it on him. Before ending these notes I must mention Rechner's and Parsons' jokes, which got to such a stage that Rechner had his patented, the patent being : (Le Gag de Corn).'

'Ready' Rechner wanted to distinguish his jokes from mine. As well as my *Alright Please* magazine I drew and circulated a comic strip called *The Adventures of Erk McQuirk*. These were single copy affairs as there were no photocopiers around in those days. I did experiment with making multiple copies from potato stamps, lino cuts and woodcuts but found them all unsatisfactory and too time consuming.

As well as being in the school choir I was also a bugler in the cadet band, attaining the rank of corporal. For the annual cadet camp we either went to Ingleburn, southwest of Sydney, or Singleton in the Hunter Valley. One year at Singleton Camp there was an outbreak of diarrhoea. The toilet block cubicles had no doors and late one night in the dark a cadet rushed in, dropped his pyjama pants and unintentionally let fly on the occupant's lap. Many didn't even make it to the toilet block. One wag changed some of the words of a popular song and 'It's all over the place...........' was soon being sung everywhere in camp.

Learning to play the bugle came in handy later when I started having trumpet lessons. However, the big drawback in camp was that I had to be up first in the morning and last to bed in the evening not counting those on piquet duty.

Whilst I was never much good at sport because I was tall and thin, I was a good sprinter. I did well in the Athletic Carnivals and was a winger in our House Rugby Union team. For a while I was also a winger in one of the North Sydney Police Boys Club Rugby League teams on Saturday mornings. In first year I played cricket in the summer. However, the following years I chose to go swimming with the school in the hot months. Over the years we swam at the Northbridge Baths, Spit Baths, Balmoral Baths and the North Sydney Olympic Pool. Although I qualified for the Life Saving Bronze Medallion, I was away at Cadet Camp when they were handed out and I don't know what happened to my one.

At the end of 1950 I passed the Intermediate Certificate exams doing best in Technical Drawing. Students had the option of continuing on to fifth year to sit for the Leaving Certificate, doing a trade course or starting work. I wasn't sure what I wanted to do for a career but reasoned there would be better opportunities if I had the Leaving Certificate. I was keen to do something in the art field but wasn't sure if I was good enough. What confidence I had was shattered by a Department of Education official who after an aptitude test told me I was unsuited for a career in art. He didn't bother to tell me what would have been a suitable occupation.

Australia has long had high standards in art especially black and white, which was my main interest. Whenever I was down near Circular Quay I would study the original artwork displayed in the window of the Bulletin Building at 252 George Street. The linework was brilliant, especially that of Norman Lindsay who worked for the Bulletin Magazine for almost fifty years. In addition to having many world-class black and white illustrators and cartoon artists, Australia had some really great comic strip artists. Jimmy Banks grew up at Normanhurst and his Ginger Meggs character was based on one of his schoolmates. It was popular in many countries around the world and syndicated in the USA as *Ginger*. Quite a few of the comic strip artists lived on the north side of the harbour and Dad told me he knew Stan Cross who drew *Wally and the Major*. Virgil Reilly lived in the next street and drew *Silver Flash, Invisible Avenger* and for a while *Chesty Bond*. I seem to remember that Stanley Pitt lived nearby also. He drew *Yarmak* but his specialty was Sci-Fi.

Rhys Williams drew various comics but is mainly remembered for his posters and landscape paintings. I have an envelope he addressed to Dad from New Guinea in 1942 with an ink sketch of a cowboy on it. He drew it with the nib and brushed the wash in with the chewed wooden handle of the pen. Emile Mercier and Alex Gurney were two of my favourite comic strip artists. In later years I lived near and got to meet Phillip Belbin who had drawn *The Raven* and the forerunner of *Air Hawk* amongst others. Phil had a miniature train ride around his property like Walt Disney.

Australian comics had their heyday in the 1940's due in large part to import and foreign exchange restrictions imposed because of the war. However, they dwindled off when US comics became available again and especially when television was introduced.

5
FISH ON FRIDAY

Whilst Mum was a Protestant and Dad was a Catholic (he didn't go to Mass) nevertheless every Friday night we had fish and chips for tea. I've heard that referring to the evening meal as 'tea' is a Highland Scottish term and that we acquired the Fish on Friday habit from the Irish Catholics.

During and after the war Dad was on shift work. One week he worked from 3pm to 11pm, the next week 11pm to 7am, then 7am to 3pm. Baby brother Bob was put to bed early which meant that on many a night there would only be Mum and me at tea time. On Fridays it was my job to go up the Crowy, buy the Women's Weekly for Mum from the Newsagent, go to the 'Swap Shop' down Willoughby Road then get the fish and chips on the way back. The 'Swap Shop' was run by two elderly sisters who sold art and craft supplies and exchanged books, magazines and comics.

There were three main types of comics; coloured American comic books, black and white Australian comic books with a coloured cover and English comics which had fewer pages and were in magazine form with text and the odd illustration. As well as the more popular American and Australian comics I enjoyed the English *Champion*. There would usually be an illustration at the start of a *Champion* story as I remember. My favourite stories were *Gusty Gale Gets Cracking* (about a schoolboy in a boarding school), *Kangaroo Kennedy* (about an Aussie cricketer living in England), *Leader of the Lost Commandos* and *Rockfist Rogan* (army and airforce stories). *Film Fun* which had panels was another favourite English comic. The English comics cost a halfpenny to swap and the others a penny. To buy new they cost threepence and sixpence respectively.

Sometimes I would buy a model aircraft kit from the sisters. In those pre-TV days we had lots of ways to amuse ourselves but drawing was my main pastime and I could listen to the wireless at the same time.

From my early teens I had various school holiday and part-time jobs. Dad was on a low wage and after the war ended there wasn't much overtime. Also by late 1949 there were five mouths to feed – Mum, Dad and three sons. I didn't mind helping out. For a while I delivered groceries on a bicycle around North Sydney for Derrin Bros. The shop was located where the MLC Building was later erected on the corner of Miller and Mount Streets. It was the old-fashioned type of grocery shop with a timber floor covered with sawdust. In the days before supermarkets a shopper would sit on an Arnotts' chair, nibble biscuits and read out their order while the grocer either weighed the item on scales and scooped it into a paper bag, or climbed a sliding ladder for tinned, bottled and packaged goods off the shelves. If desired, an order could be left at the shop and the groceries delivered that afternoon. The problem for a delivery boy in North Sydney was the hilly nature of the district. It was easy going downhill but tough going up.

Other part-time jobs I had for a while were paper boy as mentioned earlier and working on milk runs in the school holidays. Milk was usually delivered to homes in the early hours before the sun rose. One run was around St. Leonards and another was at Neutral Bay. When I was older I worked on one out the back of Dee Why. There was lots of vacant land and the blocks had wider frontages in the latter run which meant it took a lot longer to deliver all of the milk even with the milk bottled and a truck which could hold more.

With the earlier runs the milk carter and I operated from a horse and cart containing tanks of bulk milk.

'Milkos' as milkmen were called, filled a can from one of the taps at the rear of the cart and poured the householder's requirement usually into a billy can left on the front verandah. The money was mainly hidden somewhere known to the milko, such as under the doormat or under a brick in the garden. If payment was on account it would have to be posted or collected on Saturday morning where possible. As time went on milkos also delivered cream, malted milk and other dairy products.

Some nights a Government Inspector would delay us while he tested the milk to make sure it hadn't been watered down or otherwise tampered with. Having a horse who knew the route helped a lot. A milko's 'uniform' consisted of an apron, money pouch, bicycle lamp hanging from his neck and on rainy nights an oilskin and sou'wester.

One part-time job I really enjoyed was selling sweets at North Sydney Oval on Saturday afternoons in the football season. As well as being paid I was able to see the Rugby League matches. Rex Larnach-Jones operated the Tuck Shop at NSTHS, a catering business and had the concession for food and drinks at the oval in Miller Street. On Saturday afternoons us confectionery boys would load up a tray which hung by a strap from our neck with either drinks, ice cream or sweets. Rex would record the monetary value, supply us with change and off we'd go. We got paid by commission and on a good day I could earn thirty shillings. Out of that I'd buy Mum a four and sixpenny box of *Old Gold* or *Winning Post* chocolates, slip a ten shilling or £1 note under the cellophane wrapping and keep the rest for pocket money.

When I was fifteen I sometimes caught a tram into the city when I came out of school and walked up to 2GB for *Teen Time* or 2UE for *Rumpus Room*. These were afternoon wireless shows for teenagers. Hit Parade music was played and the boys and girls would be asked to comment on a particular subject, read out an advertisement on air, introduce a tune or participate in a quiz. Many radio shows had audiences and Mum had taken me to variety shows, community singing and the quiz-cum-comedies compered by Jack Davey and Bob Dyer who were top celebrities.

6
WHEN A GIRL MARRIES

When A Girl Marries was the name of a popular 'soap opera' on the wireless from 1946 to 1965. Along with others such as *Dr. Paul*, *Portia Faces Life* and *Mrs. 'Obbs* they were usually on for fifteen minutes Monday to Thursday mornings. Mum and thousands of housewives like her would listen to these so-called 'soap operas' while they dusted, scrubbed, swept, washed and ironed. I was familiar with Mum's routines from those days when I was on school holidays or at home sick. 'Soap Operas' were so named because they were mainly sponsored, or the ads were paid for, by the makers of washing soap powders such as Rinso, Persil and Lux. Big-selling headache powders like Bex and Vincent's APC's also advertised on these morning serials.

Monday was usually washing day. Before I went to school it was my job to buy a couple of empty fruit cases from the corner shop, remove the nails with a claw hammer, straighten them out and put them in the relevant nail jar in the shed. I would then chop up the wood with a tomahawk and get the fire going under the copper for Mum.

Monday was also the day our rent collector came. When my parents got married in 1934 the basic weekly wage was about £3.0s.0d and the rent for 106 was about £1.0s.0d. Mum would routinely ask the Estate Agent, Chart Abraham, about getting something fixed and he would routinely say he would ask the owner. Nothing was ever done though. The first day of the week was also traditionally the day when Mum and her neighbours scrubbed their front steps and chatted over the fence. With few labour-saving devices housework was drudgery. One consolation was that it was able to be performed in a relatively leisurely way in those days when it was rare for mothers to go out to work.

When I was very young we had a fuel stove. Mum's iron was just that, a shaped piece of iron with a handle. It had to be heated up on the stove. Meat was stored in a meat safe that hung in the wash-house. In hot weather some items had to be purchased on the day as we had neither an ice-chest nor refrigerator.

After the clothes were boiled in the copper Mum would transfer them to the tin tub with a pole. She would then soap, rub, hand-wring and rinse in cold water, place them in the clothes basket and carry them out to the clothes line. Our clothes line like most was strung between two posts with a forked-sapling prop to raise the line. Hills Hoists hadn't been invented. Mum wasn't very good at darning socks. Mine were usually lumpy on the heels where holes had been mended and re-mended causing many a blister. Also some clothing caused problems.

My woollen swim trunks used to chafe terribly between the legs. Shirts and trousers were often a size or two too big so that I would 'grow into them' and thus delay replacement. At least I didn't get hand-me-downs like my younger brothers. Don't interpret this as grumbling. It is just the way things were.

On Tuesdays Mum did the ironing and Auntie Nora came to lunch. Uncle Harry (Sparrow) and Auntie Nora lost their only child at birth. With Sparrow working nights at Luna Park, Auntie Nora would baby-sit me if Mum and Dad were going out at night. I usually played cards with her until just before my parents came home. Sometimes Auntie Nora took me out for the day when I was little. We both enjoyed going on the Manly ferries.

Often on a Wednesday Mum and her sister Girlie would catch a tram into Wynyard, shop, have lunch at Woolworths Cafeteria and go to the pictures. New releases were shown in the City before going to the suburbs and country. Whenever they took me in the school holidays I suffered the shopping but enjoyed lunch and the pictures. At the fancier cinemas there would be an orchestra, a stage show, or at the very least a Wurlitzer organ, to entertain the audience before the start and at interval. The orchestra and organ rose from below. Ice cream and confectionery could be purchased from vendors with trays walking up and down the aisles or from the Candy Bar. Sometimes on a rainy day Mum would let me wag school and go with her and Auntie Girlie.

Thursdays and Fridays were the days for more house cleaning and shopping for the basics. The retail shops were well aware that most workers got paid on those days and that was when they advertised their specials to draw customers into their shops.

Saturday morning if Dad wasn't on shift work he would accompany Mum for last-minute items and anything he required. Most shops were closed Saturday afternoons and Sundays except for milk bars and the like.

Saturday night was, following the British tradition as we understood it, bath night. We didn't have a shower at 106 until after the war. Apart from the weekly bath we 'washed' ourselves daily.

Mum always had a good sense of humour and like her parents enjoyed telling family anecdotes, some of which could be a bit embarrassing at times. One of her favourite stories was about me when I started school. Up until that time either Mum or Dad would accompany me to the backyard toilet at night and wait outside while I went. One day we had scripture class at school and that night I apparently told Mum that she needn't come up the yard as the scripture teacher said that God was watching over me. However, the following night I asked her to come with me. 'But isn't God watching over you?' she said, to which I replied, 'Yes but he might be doing something else'.

I'm not sure of the year when Mum and Dad met but Mum did tell me they had been going together for a few years when they walked over the Sydney Harbour Bridge on the day it was opened. That was 19 March 1932. Neither of them had much money when they got married because they had both been helping to support their families in the Depression. Mum had worked as a salesgirl at *The Hub* in Pitt Street then *City Fashions* near *Mark Foys* in Liverpool Street.

Mum would visit her mother and sister often when she went shopping up the Crowy. They lived two doors apart in Hume Street near where the Post Office is now located. Auntie Girlie was a good cook. Whenever I went to her place to play with my cousins Kevin and Terry she would give us home-made ginger beer and cake.

The Post Office used to be up the Pacific Highway near Shirley Road and the current location was a large paddock. There was a produce store on one corner of Hume Street and the Highway which sold things like chaff for the dwindling horse population in the district. We were fortunate in that we saw the tail-end of a way of life with horse-drawn vehicles, square-rigged sailing ships, trams and steam trains.

The row of terraces where Mum's mother and sister lived were demolished in the 1960's and replaced with a commercial office building and dance studio.

7
SHELL OIL ACQUAINTANCE

The Shell Oil Company installation at Gore Bay was officially opened on 10 June 1901. Burns Philp and Co. were the agents for NSW and Queensland and imported kerosene was the main product at first. As motor vehicles became more numerous the demand for oil and petrol rose dramatically resulting in Shell purchasing an existing refinery at Clyde in 1927. Oil tankers would discharge their loads into storage tanks at Gore Bay for transporting by barge to Clyde. The barges which were drawn by tugboats also bunkered shipping in the harbour.

Dad started with Shell as a Storeman and Packer at Gore Bay in the late 1920's. He was a quiet and serious man and rarely spoke about his early life. The majority of the workforce at the installation were employed making kerosene tins in the early years and he worked in that section initially. However, he later became a Pumpman responsible for pumping the various products from the tankers into shore tanks and then into barges. Sometimes he went on the barges to Clyde or to bunker the ships and the Flying Boats at Rose Bay.

World War 2 in the Pacific was largely about oil. In 1941 as ordered by their respective governments the American and British/Dutch oil companies suspended the supply of oil to militaristic Japan. As a consequence the Japanese invaded South-East Asia seizing the valuable oil fields, rubber plantations and other sources of raw materials.

Dad's job at that time was classified as a reserved occupation which exempted him from the armed forces. However, he was put through a security check and issued with a handgun until the war ended. Once again I only found this out years later. Sometimes he took me to work with him so I had a fair understanding of his job.

In 1962 Shell built an underground pipeline from Gore Bay to the Clyde Refinery and relocated most of the jobs to Clyde. Dad was really upset at the time as it probably would have meant moving to the Parramatta district. At the risk of losing his job he refused to be transferred. Luckily he was regarded as a valuable employee and management allowed him to remain working on the tugs and bunkering barges at Gore Bay. Later though when the tugboats were contracted out Dad quit Shell and was employed by the Tug Company where he remained until his retirement in the 1970's. He loved the harbour life.

After the war finally ended in 1945 the Social Club at Gore Bay resumed having Smokos, Balls and Children's Christmas

Parties. Two such occasions readily come to mind. One was a formal affair on a showboat one evening. The *Kalang* was a familiar sight on Sydney Harbour. Built at Chester, England in the 1920's as a car ferry, she plied between Circular Quay and the North Shore until the Harbour Bridge opened. In 1938 she was converted to a three-decker showboat and during the war served the Australian Army as a repair ship in the islands off Papua, New Guinea.

As a showboat *Kalang* could carry nearly two-thousand revellers. There was a concert, dinner and dancing on the upper deck, on the night I remember. At the end of the harbour cruise the M.C. had everyone singing 'Begin The Benzine' and 'Shell Oil Aquaintance' in lieu of the proper lyrics of Cole Porter's 'Begin The Beguine' and Robert Burns' 'Old Lang Syne', which incidentally is Scottish for 'Old Long Since'. Sadly *Kalang* ended her days in 1974 beached at Trial Bay near Kempsey on the NSW North Coast. She and two other old Sydney ferries went ashore when the tug towing them to Hong Kong lost them while carrying out repairs at sea.

The other occasion that stands out in my mind was the Children's Christmas Party cum Picnic at Clifton Gardens just after the war. Two uncles – Arnold and Horrie – also worked at Shell's Gore Bay Terminal so there were uncles, aunts, cousins and even neighbours in our picnic shed. The big surprise for the children was Father Christmas arriving in a speedboat. It may not sound impressive nowadays but in those austere times it was something to talk about. I learned later that Father Christmas was one of Dad's working and fishing mates.

The person commonly referred to as Santa Claus today was called Father Christmas when I was a child. Our British-style Father Christmas was a tall, thin figure in a long coat. I believe the popular image of Santa today originated in a 1931 Coca Cola advertisement in the USA with both Santa and the Coca Cola Company having the familiar red and white colours.

Dad was born on 16 October 1912 at Paddington NSW. Between that date and 1927 his family moved to North Sydney, Seaforth then Crows Nest. They also travelled from Sydney to Adelaide and back twice by covered wagon to visit Pa's relatives. The trips were made probably in 1925 and 1927 and took months, living off the land and earning a little money from seasonal work. With six children at the time it was hard-going. Dad had no inclination to ever travel after those trips.

One of Dad's sisters, Kath told me that when they lived in the bush at Seaforth her brother, Bill would pick and sell bunches of gumtips door-to-door to help put food on the table. Shoes were an expensive item for struggling families. One day at his North Sydney Catholic school Dad was punished for not wearing shoes. Even though he told the Brother teacher he didn't have any it made no difference. Ever since that day he had a 'thing' about shoes. His first job when he left school at about age twelve was as a shoeshine boy in the City. For years he repaired all of our shoes and got extra wear from them by adding Kromhyd rubber heels and soles.

It wasn't unusual for families to stretch the household budget by making and repairing things themselves. While listening to the wireless of an evening Mum would sew or knit. Often Dad sat at the kitchen table fixing or cleaning various items. Sometimes he would join me drawing, he was good at drawing ocean liners. There were myriad ways to make use of the time after the evening meal before TV came along.

Many a night after going to bed I would put on the headphones connected to my home-made crystal set receiver clamped to the settee I slept on and secretly listen to wireless programmes. One particular night in 1951 I woke up and finding it hard to get back to sleep I tuned in to the ABC. I couldn't believe what I heard. It was the zany humour of *The Goon Show*. I have been a fan ever since.

One law that caused many a problem was the one that stipulated hotels had to close at 6.00pm. Shell's Gore Bay installation had a fairly large workforce before the Clyde pipeline was built and many of the workers lived at Crows Nest. Most travelled to and from work on the privately-owned Greenwich Bus. When the bus reached Crows Nest going on 5 o'clock weekdays the workers would rush over to the Crows Nest Hotel and order a number of beers as the public bar was quickly filled and there was only about an hour's drinking time. It was known as the 'six o'clock swill' and looking back it was barbaric. As a consequence many a husband arrived home drunk. Dad drank in the early years of his marriage but gradually tapered off until he hardly ever had a drink. Mainly he drank beer but now and then he had a rum. He got the rum from the oil tanker crews.

Dad died of bladder cancer in 1994 aged 81. He had been a smoker and that, plus his occupation was the probable cause.

8
JUST FOR FUN

Sydney's Luna Park opened on 4 October 1935, fifteen days after I was born. The site had previously been the construction factory of Dorman Long, the contractors who built the Sydney Harbour Bridge. Prior to that it had been a railway station. Luna Park took up about 2.25 hectares and a good crowd was six to eight thousand fun-seekers. On New Years Eve it was about fourteen thousand.

Uncle Harry who like his father was nicknamed Sparrow, had been a seaman and had lost his first wife, ran the games at Luna Park. Before that he had also been a taxi driver and for a time owned a fish and chip shop in West Street, Crows Nest. The games were run as a concession by David Atkins (DA) the Manager and one of the owners of Luna Park. Sparrow worked at the Park during the day ordering stock and replenishing the stands with prizes that were packaged and dressed by his team of ladies. The novelties, chocolates, kewpie dolls, etc., given away as prizes were mostly purchased in bulk. He also supervised the games staff at night and on weekends when the Park was open. He and Auntie Nora lived in a flat above a butcher shop in Alfred Street, the street that leads down to Luna Park from North Sydney.

Being one of the bosses Sparrow was usually able to arrange employment for family members when requested. There were about forty permanent 'day staff' made up of carpenters, cleaners, electricians, fitters, painters and so on in addition to management and the office staff.

The 'night staff' mostly had daytime jobs outside Luna Park. Having a second job gave them the opportunity to earn extra money to pay off a house, car or whatever. They numbered in the hundreds.

At the end of the school year in 1951 I was able to get holiday work at Luna Park through Sparrow. I started off working on the games as a gamesboy but after a while transferred to the rides.

On the night staff we worked over thirty hours a week and earned good money for those days. Sometimes the Park stayed open until well after midnight paying us penalty rates. The first time I worked on the rides I was assigned to the *Merry-go-Round*. It was a 1910 American Charles Carmel Carousel with a 1915 German organ pumping out music in the manner of a pianola. As an attendant I had to wear my own white shirt, a tie and dark trousers. Luna Park supplied a red and gold peaked cap with a white cover and a khaki coat with red piping and cuffs, affectionately called 'a zookeepers coat'. The cashiers and games staff wore smocks.

The *Carousel* crew consisted of a female cashier in the ticket box, a charge-hand who operated the controls and two junior attendants who collected the tickets once the ride was going and who also helped riders on and off when necessary. That first day was a Saturday and I worked two shifts from 1.30pm until about 1.30am with a few tea breaks and a meal break. When I finally got home to bed the room started spinning and I had to race outside to be sick.

One of the newer attractions was *Davy Jones Locker* located near the *Carousel.* There were various illusions inside one of which was a skull that appeared to change into a live woman's head on a spider web. I got to know the girl who provided the head and used to pop over and chat with her occasionally when I had a break. On this particular night she asked me to watch things while she went to the ladies toilet. The attendant came into the viewing room when a crowd had built up and went into his spiel.

'Ladies and gentlemen, boys and girls, if you watch the skull carefully you will see it transform into a beautiful, live woman's head. Speak to her, ask her questions and she will answer you.'

Lilly hadn't returned so being a joker I pressed the buttons which dimmed one light and gradually illuminated another so that my head could be seen by the audience instead of the plaster skull. As I appeared there were loud protests from the crowd.

‘Have you had a sex change luv?’

‘If that’s a beautiful girl I’m a monkey’s uncle.’

As the comments came thick and fast I pressed the lighting buttons and spoke into the microphone in my best ghostly voice:

‘Farewell, I must go o o o o, goodbye e e e e.’

Luckily for the show Lilly came back at that moment and took over.

New Year’s Eve was the big night of the year at Luna Park. As well as the games and rides, the *Palais de Danse* which was a covered concrete pontoon with a dance floor and Luna Park’s own dance band, attracted a large following. At midnight there was a fireworks display, revellers kissed perfect strangers and groups of people joined hands singing ‘Auld Lang Syne’. The Park stayed open most of the night. It was a fun job.

All too soon it was time to go back to school for my final year. However, it was not to be. With the board I paid Mum while working in the holidays she had been able to balance the weekly household budget. In January 1952 Bob had turned nine and Johnny was a two year-old. For me to go back to high school for another year would have been financially difficult for Mum. She asked me if I would mind not going back. At the time I still wasn’t sure what I wanted to do when I finished fifth year. I had really enjoyed working at Luna Park so I asked DA if there was a full-time position available and he said that I could start in the office as Office Boy. I accepted and reported at 8.30am the following Monday. Mum was relieved.

The job of office boy consisted of mundane tasks such as date-stamping complimentary tickets, assisting with emptying the Penny Arcade slot machines, sorting and counting the coins then rolling them up in bolts ready for banking. In addition to DA and Ted (Hoppy) Hopkins the Park's Engineer and one of the owners, the office staff comprised Mr. Baxter the Company Secretary, Miss Johnson the shorthand typist and Mr. Cochrane who handled the money. I was so bored with the job I used to daydream like Walter Mitty and one time when I was date-stamping tickets I got up to about the 47th of February before I woke up. On the seventh of that month while I was working on the night staff Hoppy announced over the public address system that King George VI had died and as a mark of respect Luna Park was closing immediately.

After a few weeks I took a portfolio of my art into DA and asked him if I could work with Luna Park's artist, Arthur (Art) Barton and his crew. DA was a paternalistic boss and I think he fancied himself as akin to the Hollywood Studio bosses such as Louis B. Mayer. He had been to Hollywood and had lots of kitsch in his office which overlooked the Midway. One piece I particularly admired was a large framed picture of a scene from Walt Disney's *Snow White And The Seven Dwarfs*. It featured the dwarfs' cottage in the woods with a shaft of sunlight shining on it through the trees. DA put his arm around my shoulder as was his habit with staff and said he would speak to Arthur.

What eventuated was I became a trainee, working initially with Charlie Kinninburg the Park's signwriter. It wasn't an apprenticeship but good enough. The bad news was my day job pay went down, but with my night staff earnings I was still doing well. Arthur Barton had assessed my art portfolio and his opinion was that I was more illustrator than fine artist. Arthur had started off as a signwriter, served in World War I then studied art in London at the Slade School if I remember correctly. Settling in Sydney on his return he created Christmas scenes in department store windows, was a sketch artist, illustrated books and drew comics before working at Luna Park when it was being built and afterwards.

Some people looked down on Arthur's Luna Park murals saying they resembled the art on English seaside postcards. That was so but he painted them that way deliberately. I saw some of his watercolours and they were masterful. Before an attraction was built he would depict it in watercolour and I watched as he painted two huge oil portraits of Elizabeth and Philip in 1952 to celebrate Elizabeth's accession to the throne. The portraits were hung on the front of the Coney Island Funnyland building. Around that time he also painted a giant penny for the entrance to the Penny Arcade. Not bad for a man with one glass eye.

There was another worker with a glass eye at Luna Park. When he'd had a few too many drinks he would take it out, put it on someone's shoulder and say, 'I've got my eye on you'. The place was full of characters. My grandfather Pa was one of those characters. During the winter close-down he worked as a casual repairing canvas awnings and the mats used on the slides. From his seafaring days he had a set of sail needles and knew about knots and sailmaker's whipping. He would sit in a sunny corner down near *Coney Island* and tell me stories about when he was a pirate. It was a load of bull but he was such a good yarn spinner it didn't matter.

One day when I went up the Crowy on an errand there was a crowd watching a fight outside the Crows Nest Hotel. Pa was fighting some other bloke. He would have been about seventy-three at the time. My cousin Sylvia told me that one time he was sitting down in his backyard talking to a mate while he was babysitting one of his grandchildren. Noticing that the little fellow had dirtied his nappy, Pa casually reached over and pulled it down. He then grabbed the nearby garden hose and hosed both his grandchild's bottom and the nappy while still talking to his friend.

Dick was one of the senior maintenance staff at the Park who whenever we were passing each other on the Midway would say to me, 'G'day young Ronnie, are you getting any?'

I never seemed to have a satisfactory reply to that so one day I got in first in order to put him on the spot.

'G'day Dick, are you getting any?' I said as he approached.

'Enough to keep the rust off it,' he replied as he strode by.

The painters quarters were underneath the stairs next to the North Sydney Olympic Pool. Besides Arthur and Charlie there was Arthur's offsider, 'Tich' Finey a Kiwi whose uncle was George Finey, a well-known artist. Last but not least was Fred

Switely who was also the trumpet playing band leader of the Luna Park Dance Band. Any major painting work was carried out by painting contractors.

The tasks I was given included rubbing down the wooden cabinets of ancient 'What The Butler Saw' type slot machines before re-varnishing; painting or spraying over repairs to a variety of rides; re-painting handrails and signwriting. There were also some more unusual jobs such as helping to repair the famous face at the entrance and making giant clown heads to be worn in parades.

One Friday afternoon just as I started to change out of my overalls prior to bundying off and collecting my week's pay, Harry Holland the foreman rushed in and asked me to get some paint and cover over some plaster repairs to figures in the *River Caves*. Everyone else had already gone so I mixed up the colours, grabbed a brush and raced off.

To get to the scene in the Caves I started the water wheel briefly, hopped into a boat and let the current take me there. In my haste I forgot to moor the boat at the scene and by the time I'd painted over the repairs the boat had drifted away. I called out but there was no response. As a last resort I could've waded out but luckily I found there was a ladder inside a fake hollow tree which allowed me to exit at the foot of a dip in the *Big Dipper*.

Because I was the youngest member of the day staff it was my job to get the lunch orders from a sandwich shop opposite Milsons Point Railway Station. Mum usually made my lunch and at lunchtime I either fished off the side of the *Palais de Danse* or ate with my workmates before going down to the giant slides in *Coney Island.* Now and then I arrived early on the weekends and went for a swim in the Olympic Pool next to the Park. In winter Luna Park was closed to the public while major maintenance work was carried out and any new attractions installed. The day staff also took their two weeks annual leave during that period.

Early in 1953 my night staff job had me operating an electronic shooting gallery on the harbour side of the *Carousel.* Although it was operated by Luna Park it was a concession owned by two Poms. Bernie and Ron were a couple of sharp Cockney businessmen. It appeared since I had taken over running their gallery the takings had increased dramatically. When it was quiet I used to put on a shooting display to attract customers.

The guns weren't exactly accurate and needed regulating on a dial, especially on hot days. The nearby *Carousel* was decorated with hundreds of small round mirrors which sometimes fell off. My trick was to turn the dial up for the guns, hold up one of the mirrors and shoot with my back to the targets. A bell would ring with each hit and I would get a bullseye every time. I would then turn the dial back and rake in the money from the eager shooters.

Bernie and Ron also had a pie run. In those days hotels didn't have counter lunches like they do now. The two Poms saw the opportunity and arranged to sell pies in a number of hotels between Taylor Square and Botany. They rigged up an old Ford V8 panel van with car batteries and pie ovens and did a deal with a pastrycook at Dover Heights who had won awards at the Easter Show for the best meat pies.

After establishing the business they talked two of us from Luna Park into working for them. The bait was that for only a few hours work six days a week we would earn more money than we did at the Park. Whilst I enjoyed working at Luna, apart from two weeks annual leave I'd worked long hours every day for fifteen months. Also I was doing all the donkey painting jobs and opportunities to be creative were rare. I had no social life outside of the job and hardly any leisure time. By coincidence the other Luna Park employee they recruited was also named Ron. He worked on the games, was married and owned a car. Married Ron would give me a lift over to the shop at Dover Heights of a morning where we'd meet the two Poms and load the van with pies. They would drop us off at various locations where there were a few pubs near one another, go off to their allocated ones, return and repeat the process. We usually finished the run just after 2pm on weekdays and on Saturdays we worked until 6pm calling back to each pub a few times.

Wearing an apron and carrying a cane clothes basket full of hot pies we did the rounds of the bars and moved on. My patter went like this; 'Hot meat pies, hot meat pies, have a curry in a hurry, or a potato later, hot meat pies.'

Some customers insisted on handing me a beer not realising I was under age. After we'd finished for the day Married Ron or Bernie and Ron would drop me off in the City. Feeling tired if I'd had a beer, I'd often go to a newsreel theatre or a cinema that ran continuous sessions, sometimes falling asleep. Up in the gods at the Palace Cinema near Adam's Marble Bar when it was in Pitt Street was where I mostly went.

Knowing Mum and Dad wouldn't approve of the job I stretched the truth and told them I was working for a pastrycook at Dover Heights. My parents enjoyed any leftover pies I sometimes took home.

Veronica Parsons née Crowe

Thomas Parsons

Violet Wales Mitchell née Pollock

William George Mitchell

Thelma Pearl Parsons
née Mitchell
and
Ronald Thomas Parsons Snr.

Ronald Thomas Parsons Jnr. and parents c 1938

Robert Vincent Parsons

John William Parsons

106 Backyard 1947

Class 1A Lady Hay School 1942 – Author fifth from left, back row

Cadet Camp Ingleburn 1949

Sunday Outing 1951

Sketch by Author at age 15

Tut and me, ANZAC Rifle Range 1954

Genevieve, Narrabeen Lakes 1955

Greenmount Guest House, Easter 1955 – Author third from right, back row centre.

Woolworths, Liverpool Street staff 1956 – Author third from right, back row as usual.

NASHO DAZE

NASHO DAZE

NASHO DAZE

9
GONE BUSH

By the time it was approaching Easter I'd had enough of the pie business. I contacted DA and told him I was available to work at the Easter Show if he wanted me. As long as you were hard-working and honest they would always take you back on at Luna Park. It was a convenient way to earn extra money when required.

DA had games and rides at The Royal Agricultural Show and the Brisbane Ekka. I commenced at the showground at Moore Park before the Show opened helping to dress the games and readying the *Laff in the Dark*, which was a ghost train ride. Another showman had the ghost train name. For the duration of the Show I worked, ate and slept at the showground. I worked on the games and *Laff in the Dark* and after the Show closed at night I slept on the floor of the *Laughing Clowns* game to ensure the prizes weren't pilfered.

Occasionally I was also a spruiker for the games. Wearing a striped blazer and a straw boater and holding a cane with a curved handle I would approach a couple and hook the bloke under the arm. If it was a young bloke and his girlfriend I'd say, 'C'mon Billy bring your Missus over and win her a prize'. If it was an older married couple I'd say, 'C'mon Billy bring your girlfriend over and win her a prize'. It hardly ever failed to get them in.

The facade of the *Laff in the Dark* was a King Kong-like ape's head painted by Arthur Barton. The carriages departed and returned through doors at the corners of the huge mouth. Uniformed attendants bundled riders through day and night. Attendance at the Show at that time averaged 100,000 a day. If things did get quiet on the *Laff* one of us would don a gorilla suit and draw a crowd by scaring riders as their carriage came out. They would think it was over as they crashed through the door only to find a gorilla spring out at them. The crowd loved it but it was not so good for the staff. You wouldn't believe the number of times we had to clean the seats after riders had wet themselves.

Possibly due to all the westerns I'd seen at the cinema I had a love of horses. A number of times I'd gone riding with mates at Narrabeen Lakes. There was a riding school where you could hire horses by the hour, half or full day. We usually rode around the lake as far as Deep Creek. I was also fond of sketching horses. When I had the opportunity at the Show I'd go down to the stables and mix with the country people. Many of them camped in the lofts or next to the horse stalls while the Show was on. Some sang and played the guitar. I was not to know it would have an influence on my life in the near future.

After the Show ended I looked through the Positions Vacant column of the Sydney Morning Herald for a job closer to home. Believing I had some talent as a salesman I applied for and got a job with Woolworths at Chatswood. I was seventeen at the time and still wasn't sure what I wanted to do for a career. That's where I met Tex. I don't remember his real name. He told me to call him by his nickname Tex so I did.

Tex was the same age as me and lived further up the North Shore. He used to tell me stories about working on a cattle property in western Queensland. I didn't know if he had, or was making it up, but I'd do a Walter Mitty and see myself heading off stampedes and catching cattle duffers.

One day at work he said he was going up to Queensland again and then on to Darwin.

'How about coming with me Lofty?' Lofty was what he called me. Tex was short and tubby.

'I'll ask my parents', I replied assuming Tex had his parents' permission.

When I asked Mum she told me to ask my father. Dad said, 'No!'.

He had a Victorian-era attitude regarding family. Although I hounded him day after day he wouldn't budge. So Tex and I gave notice, purchased some gear at an army disposal shop and booked two seats on the night mail train to Kempsey where Tex had an aunt. On the day, I left a note for Mum and Dad and caught an electric train from St. Leonards to Central Railway Station.

Unbeknownst to me Tex had also been refused permission by his parents and left a note. I found out later that at about 9 o'clock that night there was a knock on the door at 106. Dad was already in bed so Mum answered it. Tex's parents introduced themselves and showed Mum their son's note. We didn't have a telephone. Mum invited them in and they promptly sat on the side of the bed and discussed the matter with Dad. It was decided not to take any action for the time being.

We arrived in Kempsey early the next day and called on Tex's relative. We told her we were making our way up to Queensland and the Northern Territory. His Aunt gave us a meal after which we walked along the Pacific Highway to the northern end of town to thumb a lift. We only got as far as Eungai Rail by nightfall so we had a snack and camped by the side of the road.

Early next morning we saw there was a farmhouse nearby. Taking a billycan with us we headed for the house intending to ask for some hot water as it was too damp to light a fire. As we reached the verandah two vicious-looking dogs came around the side of the house and made for us. We pounded on the front door which opened just as the dogs reached us. The lady yelled at the dogs and they slunk off.

When we explained our situation she invited us to have breakfast with her, her husband and sister-in-law.

'Wait in the lounge room and I'll call you when breakfast is ready', she said.

There was a hallway which led to the lounge room and the timber floor sloped upwards to it. The front wooden stumps had apparently sunk down. There was no ceiling and we noticed a possum looking down on us from a rafter as we sat on an ancient horsehair-filled sofa.

The walls were lined with framed sepia photographs of young World War I diggers we assumed to be family members. When breakfast was ready we stepped down into the dining room which was a dirtfloor lean-to with a long table made of saplings.

The husband didn't speak as we ate our porridge. Neither did his sister who was obviously simple-minded. After a cup of tea we said we'd best be going and at the front door as the lady shooed the dogs away again we offered to pay for the breakfast, as they were not exactly well off. However, she wouldn't accept anything so we thanked her and went on our way.

We made it to Ballina that day. Just on sunset the clergyman who had given us the last lift dropped us off near a church on the outskirts. We unrolled our swags in the graveyard but after a while had second thoughts. Tex suggested we walk to the Police Station and ask if we could bed down in an empty cell for the night. Which we did. Our money had to be conserved until we got temporary work.

It was late again and pitch black when we arrived on the Gold Coast. We thanked the driver and got our gear off the back of the truck. Feeling tired and grubby we crossed the road and hit the sack in what we thought was a small clearing. Next morning we were awakened by two policemen as traffic whizzed past us on both sides. We had unknowingly flaked out on the wide median strip of a dual carriageway. After patiently listening to our story they drove us to a shopping centre and told us where we might find some work. Shortly afterwards Tex and I had our first disagreement.

From the outset we had agreed to pool our money and share in case only one of us got work. Tex said he was going for a walk. When he came back I noticed he was wearing an expensive-looking new belt. He had spent nearly all of the money we had left on it. Luckily we both got work gardening that morning and managed to find cheap temporary accommodation. It was off-season.

A week later we set off for Ipswich. We sought and got employment at the Queensland Woollen Mills at North Ipswich. However, accommodation was scarce. Tex got a shared room close to the Ipswich town centre. I had to go further afield to Booval. In retrospect it was good to have a break from one another outside of work.

I had my own room in a boarding house which was an old Queenslander on the main road. The only other boarder was an Italian migrant who seemed to spend most of his spare time photographing himself and posing in front of a mirror. To get to work I had to catch a train from Booval to Ipswich then walk across the bridge over the Bremer River to the mills. It was monotonous work feeding old army blankets and such into machines that washed, shredded and so forth until the wool was in a reusable form.

The one luxury we allowed ourselves was going to the pictures. There were two cinemas we went to in Ipswich. The *Wintergarten* was a beautiful theatre in the middle of town. The other one was down in a dip of the highway on the Brisbane side. It had a flat concrete floor and patrons sat in deck chairs. At the end of each session the ushers came around waking the many people who had fallen asleep. Smoking was permitted while the film was on and the picture had to be looked at through a haze of smoke.

Our time at Ipswich was uneventful and soon we were headed west to Charleville. However, we never got there. Hitchhiking along the old Ipswich - Toowoomba road it was hot during the day but cold at night when we camped. For the section from Helidon up the range to Toowoomba we caught one of Jack McCafferty's then black, cream and orange coloured buses. Spending a couple of days in the Garden City little did I know that forty years later I would make it my home.

As had become our habit we positioned ourselves on the side of the highway on the outskirts of town and soon hitched a ride. Hitchhiking wasn't considered that dangerous in the early 1950's. A grazier driving a fairly new American Nash sedan gave us a lift. By the time we passed through Oakey we had agreed to work for him for a month. He'd been an officer in the Australian army during World War 2 and owned a soldier settlement property in brigalow country north-west of Chinchilla. He told us he had run sheep during the Korean War wool boom but was changing over to cattle. Tex and I were to assist him strengthening the fence around the boundary of the property for full board and a wage. That suited us as we would be able to save our wages.

Our accommodation was an old farmhouse being used as a store for feed and we ate at the main residence some distance away. Just after sunrise we would walk up to the homestead and carry out a few chores while the boss's wife got breakfast ready. I had to milk the house cow and saddle up the children's ponies which they rode to school. Tex had to chop the firewood. After breakfast the three of us would drive out to the section of fence where we'd be working. Sundays were the only days we had off. That's when we washed our clothes and so on.

One morning the boss asked me to have a go at felling a tree. As well as working on the fence he was clearing a track just inside the boundary so that he could drive around the property. I knew what to do so that the big gum would fall away from the fence but just as it started to fall a sudden gust of wind blew it back flattening the fence. I should point out that all I had was an axe, muscle and sweat. We didn't have chainsaws like nowadays. That same day a big mob of kangaroos suddenly came bounding towards us. I stood my ground thinking they would veer off but the boss yelled at me to get behind a tree. He was right they just kept coming at us.

There was a bulldozer contractor doing some clearing on a neighbouring property and the boss arranged with the contractor, Andy, to work on the perimeter track after he finished his current job. Andy was a tall, wiry bloke with sandy hair. He wore a check shirt and old army drill pants and went barefooted. He probably had trouble finding footwear to fit him for he had the longest feet I've ever seen in all my life.

To save time going back to the homestead for lunch the missus would pack cut lunches for us in an ex-army ammo tin. While Andy was working for the boss the missus made lunch for him too. On the first day he joined us it was very hot and dry and

Andy was covered in dust. We usually sat down and opened the greaseproof paper on our laps but Andy placed his sandwiches on the ground and used the wrapping as a bib. The boss said, 'Andy', and pointed to the sandwiches in the dirt. The boss was very well mannered. We then watched in amazement as Andy mumbled, 'Oh, sorry', and moved his sandwiches onto a dried cow pat, using it as a plate.

I had two hairy experiences during that time. One hot afternoon I had the job of picking up any sticks left on the ground behind Andy's bulldozer. The boss didn't want anything flying up from the new track and damaging the underside of his car. Bored and half asleep in the heat I almost picked up a death adder. That sure woke me up.

The second episode occurred at knock off time one day. The boss, Tex and yours truly had walked out to where we were stringing wire and moved further and further away from the homestead. The boss didn't feel like walking all the way home, so he fashioned a snaffle bridle with a single rein from fencing wire and put it on a horse that was grazing nearby. He told me to hop aboard, ride back to the stable, saddle up and return with two extra mounts.

I had no sooner got on when he slapped the horse's rump and off I went hanging on like grim death. The really hairy part came when we jumped across a dried-up creek bed with a fallen tree angled across it. I didn't see it until it was too late as I was leaning forward. In any case the horse seemed to know best what to do, thankfully.

All too soon the month was up. We said our goodbyes to the

missus and especially the children whom we had gotten to know well. The boss kindly drove us to Dalby as we had decided to go up the Queensland coast then head west to Mt. Isa and along the Barkly Highway to the Northern Territory.

10
ON THE ROAD AGAIN

From Dalby we hitchhiked north to Bell on our way to Murgon where we planned to catch a train down to the coast. When we reached Bell I suddenly realised it was September 19, my birthday. I was eighteen so we promptly made for the pub to celebrate. Tex ordered two glasses of red wine and we sat down at a table in an old-fashioned room with a fireplace and log fire. He started acting the goat pretending to be an English aristocrat. I joined in and we got really sozzled. When it came closing time we tossed our empty glasses over our shoulders into the fireplace then staggered across the road to an open-sided grain shed and hit the sack.

Shortly after I was awakened by a light shining in my face. It appeared the publican had mentioned our little sojourn to the local policeman, who let us sleep in the empty lock-up after we apologised and paid for the broken glasses. Some country cops used a lot of common sense when dealing with misbehaviour.

The next day we reached Murgon and purchased tickets for the train down to Maryborough on the coast. I don't know if it was because we both had hangovers, but we had our second altercation over money. Tex was diddling me again. It came to push and shove but we stopped when we saw we were upsetting an elderly couple who were also waiting on the station platform.

At Maryborough we jumped a rattler and hid under a tarpaulin in a wagon half full of timber until we reached Rockhampton, where we decided not to press our luck and purchased tickets to Ayr on the Sunlander. Tex reckoned he had relatives at Ayr but we couldn't locate them. However, we did manage to get temporary employment at the nearby Pioneer Sugar Mills. It was the hardest physical work I've ever done. The mills were operating around the clock and there were three eight-hour shifts. I didn't know it then but Russell Drysdale, one of my favourite Australian painters, was a director of the sugar mills at Pioneer.

The cane was brought in on a narrow gauge railway and dumped down a hole onto a conveyor belt that took it up for crushing. A lot of cane would slip down the sides of the belt, so to prevent it from clogging up there was a concreted room underneath where one or two workers pitchforked any fallen cane onto a smaller conveyor belt. It was very hot and humid and we wore only shorts, socks and boots. The worst part was every so often we'd get speared in the back by a length of sugar cane. It rarely drew blood but it hurt. It got so you'd be anticipating it happening whenever a fresh load hit the main conveyor belt.

Early one morning just before I was due to finish my shift – I was working solo – the foreman came down and asked if I'd work through the next shift as my relief worker was ill. I reluctantly agreed and was completely knackered when the sixteen hours were up. The mills had their own single men's quarters and canteen. I crawled into my bed and slept like the sleep of the dead. We only worked there for a few weeks but I was glad to leave, partly on account of the smell of the crushed cane which I disliked intensely.

Back at Ayr we caught a train to Townsville then another one out to Charters Towers. There was no work for us there so we caught the train to Mt. Isa. Depending on metal prices, demand, etc., sometimes there are lots of jobs available in mining towns and at other times there aren't. We arrived at a time when the big Mt. Isa mine was not taking on new workers. We asked around and someone suggested we might get work at one of the gold mines near Tennant Creek. That was when Tex dropped a bombshell. He told me that he was going back to Sydney to work and save enough money to go to America. Our friendship had gone stale by that time so I wished him luck and set off for the Northern Territory. I had planned to go to Darwin and that's what I was going to do.

I got a lift on a semi to Camooweal near the Queensland/ Northern Territory border that day. It was like a town in a Hollywood western. There was a hotel at each end of the main street and there were hitching rails outside. My first port of call was the town's cafe. It was teatime and I was famished. The walls were corrugated iron with hessian drapes and like the farmhouse back at Eungai Rail the cafe had a dirt floor and tables made of saplings. I think I ordered steak and eggs and a mug of tea. That first night in Camooweal I camped down near what looked like a billabong or part of the Georgina River.

The next morning I woke up late to the sound of nearby voices. It was some local aborigines camped not far away. Even though the water was a brown colour it looked inviting and I was pretty grubby. I stripped down to my boxer shorts and waded out to a half-submerged old water tank. The bottom was ankle-deep mud but out past the tank it was deep enough to swim. Some of the blackfellas came along and were diving off the tank and having a whale of a time.

After my swim I sat on the tank and got talking to a couple of them. I think they were of the Kalkadoon tribe. All of a sudden they all became quiet and still. A whole lot of pelicans came down and settled on the water. One of the swimmers appeared to slowly drift over to a big pelican then like greased lightning reached out and grabbed it by the neck and a leg to a roar of approval. I was invited to lunch and dined on pelican stew which they cooked in an old kero tin.

About five o'clock I was having a drink in the Post Office Hotel when I was approached by a fencing contractor. He'd had a barney with his offsider and wanted to know if I'd like to help him until he got a permanent replacement. He was working at Austral Downs station about a hundred kilometres south-west of Camooweal on the Northern Territory side of the border. I agreed and we shook hands on it. He said we wouldn't be leaving until Sunday and asked where I was staying. When I told him my circumstances he said he would pay for my accommodation and meals at that pub and gave me a fiver as an AAW (advance against wages).

For the next few days I explored outside the town, swam, played billiards and read paperback novels. On the day before we were due to leave the fencer told me he'd made up with his offsider and wouldn't need me. He was very apologetic and gave me another fiver. I didn't mind. It was the easiest ten quid I ever earned.

As strange as it may seem after lunch I managed to get a lift with a bloke who'd just taken delivery of a new MG and was going for a drive. The road from Mt. Isa to Tennant Creek had been sealed during World War 2 as had the road from Alice Springs to Darwin. He dropped me off at a bore about ninety kilometres out saying I'd probably pick up a semi in the late afternoon or early evening. I had a meal of sardines on Sao biscuits and a mug of tea made from the bore water at about six o'clock.

No vehicles came along from either direction for three days. I had what was referred to locally as 'chatty' water from the bore but no more food. To fill in the time and keep my mind occupied I started off just whittling but after a while found myself carving a fork. I took my time and made a good job of it. When a ute finally came along I had my wooden knife, fork and spoon all ready. I had enough nous to know not to stray from the water, but it had occurred to me that I might perish.

When I heard the sound of a vehicle coming from the direction of Camooweal I ran onto the road waving my arms. It turned out to be a middle-aged couple in a circa 1926 Chrysler utility. When I explained my predicament they pulled over and I helped the driver set up camp while his wife got our tea ready. It was late in the day and they had been looking for a place to stop over-night anyway. My prayers had been answered for they told me there was over a hundred quid's worth of food in the back of the ute.

During the meal I learned they were from Melbourne and were driving up to Wyndham to work. Red, as he was known, was an ex-boxer and I quickly found out they were metho-drinkers. He talked me into trying it, but I only had a sip. Apparently you start off with mainly water then gradually increase the proportion of methylated spirits.

After lunch the next day Red let me drive while they both dozed off. Dad had shown me how to drive a car and after getting used to changing the gears it was easy as the road was fairly straight and flat. All was going well until it appeared we were catching up to the horizon. Suddenly we were going down a steep slope and the footbrake was virtually useless. The road twisted and turned but I managed to get us to the bottom in one piece. I stopped and rolled a cigarette to settle my nerves and looked around. We were in what seemed like an ancient meteorite crater. After a smoke I hopped back in and drove across to the other side and up the hill. Red and his missus slept through it all.

The following day we had a breakdown. There was a hole in the engine block and the water was leaking out. I sharpened a stick and Red glued it in with *Tarzan's Grip*. It worked. While we were stopped a couple of vehicles came along. It was an

American anthropological expedition. There were three men and a woman who were in Australia to study the Aborigines. The young woman had film star looks and was wearing a pink-checked blouse and tight jeans. I'd only seen blue jeans in films before. They offered assistance but we told them we had things under control. However, we did travel in convoy with them until we were confident the plug would hold. When we reached Tennant Creek I parted with Red and his wife. Their drinking and arguments were too much for me. They even wanted to adopt me.

The township of Tennant Creek was actually some distance away from the Creek itself. Water was trucked in by a firm called Ford Bros. if my memory serves me correctly. Consequently you had to pay for a glass of water. They used Second World War blitz wagons with tanks on them to cart the water. There was no work available in the gold mines or the township but I managed to get a job of sorts. A truckie gave me a lift to Darwin in return for acting as offsider on the trip. I think he was also pleased to have company on the long drive. During my travels I was frequently nicknamed *Snowy* or *Lofty*.

We left in a convoy which was not uncommon in the Territory as distances between settlements were great and there wasn't much traffic in the event of a serious breakdown. Also there were no CB radios, or mobile phones in 1953. The prime mover was a Perkins diesel and it was doubly hot in the cabin with the engine cowling in between us. At one place we stopped at it was 126°F (52°C). We downed two large bottles of warm soft drink each.

Now and then a semi in front of us would start to swerve from side to side then suddenly go bush. The other drivers would sound their horns and the straying driver would stop, get out of his vehicle and pour water from a canvas water bag over his head to wake himself up. At the top of a hill south of Darwin we stopped for a meal at a place called *The Tank and Tummy Station*. In the window they had prospector gear for sale consisting of an ex-army haversack with some tools and ore samples. There was a lot of prospecting going on in Northern Australia for uranium at that time. If I'd wanted to I had an opportunity to go prospecting in the north-west with Johannson of road train fame.

Eventually we arrived in Darwin and I caught sight of the Timor Sea. I helped with the unloading and thanked the driver. When I asked him about a place to camp he suggested Mindil Beach.

11
THE TOP END

I was surprised when I got to Mindil Beach to find an old band rotunda in parkland. I decided to camp in the rotunda that night but first a swim in the ocean was the order of the day. Because they have big tides up north I had to wade out a long way to where it was deep enough to swim in the calm water. There was no one else on the beach when I dived in but while I was doing a few laps I heard someone calling out. A bloke was yelling at me to come ashore. When I got back to the beach he told me there were poisonous Portuguese Man-of-War jellyfish and sea wasps about and if I wanted to swim to go around to Lameroo Baths. I shuddered because there had been numerous jelly blubbers swimming around me.

The following morning I rose early, cleaned myself up as best I could and after hiding my kit bag walked up to the town centre.

Darwin was different to all the other places I'd been. For a start being up in the tropics it felt different. The flora was different and I'd never seen anything like some of the houses. Many were up on tall stumps like old Queenslanders but the walls comprised rows of fibro louvres. Some of the buildings such as the Bank of New South Wales still showed signs of the Japanese air attacks on Darwin with lines of bullet holes from strafing on the outside. Remember this was only eight years after WW2. Altogether the Darwin area was attacked from the air about sixty-four times I heard.

In the front of one house there was a sign that brought a smile to my face. The sign read, 'Send your soles to heaven. Les Heaven, Shoe Repairs'. Further along there was a hut with a sign on the roof identifying it as 'The Coola-Bar Refreshments'. I stopped there and asked for a strawberry milk shake.

'Powdered or goat's?' the bloke behind the counter replied.

This was all new to me. He explained it was too hot for cows hence the alternatives. I was down to my last ten shilling note which I'd kept in my boot for such an emergency, so I played it safe and ordered a powdered milk shake. Goat's milk is a lot richer than cow's milk and more apt to go sour. Mum had often given us powdered milk when she ran out of cow's milk. By coincidence at about that time Mum and Dad were getting their first 'fridge.

I had written home a few times to let the family know where I was and that I was OK. However, at my request I'd not received word from them because of the uncertainty of my movements. I got a job that day as a labourer with the then Department of Civil Aviation (DCA) so I wrote home providing a return address. When a reply came a week or so later Mum advised they'd purchased a 'Silent Knight' refrigerator and she was making home-made ice cream.

The DCA had it's own quarters for the mostly single male employees. Located in the Parap area it had previously been a military camp I think and had a canteen. They put my name down for accommodation but told me there wouldn't be a vacancy for a little while. There was a rubbish tip nearby with a lot of rusting car bodies so I made a mattress of sorts using car seats in one and stowed my gear in the boot. Until I got a shared room in the camp I slept in the car and used the camp's facilities to wash and eat. I was broke and didn't have much choice.

Assigned to a labouring gang, the work involved dismantling WW2 metal structures at a disused airstrip south of Darwin. The Northern Territory was under the administration of the Commonwealth Government back then. There were no local or territory governments. It was the same in the A.C.T. The Federal Government gained my respect for the way they avoided waste. The structures we were dismantling were of corrugated iron bolted to angle-iron frames on concrete pads. We had to unbolt the corrugated iron and frames for re-use. The following year when I did my National Service training, some of our clothing and equipment was from WW1, including our .303 rifles. It had been cleaned and put in storage after the wars. The Government Departments responsible deserved full marks for being careful with the taxpayers' money.

Some days we were driven out to Nightcliff to load trucks with sand. There were no bobcats, we had to toss the sand up and over with a shovel. It was 1953 and I remember shovelling sand at Nightcliff on Melbourne Cup day. *Nodalla* won at fourteen to one, *Hydrogen* the favourite failed to win a place.

A fortnight later I cut my shin on a rusty sheet of corrugated iron. I stuck a band-aid over it and forgot about it. However, it quickly developed into a tropical ulcer. I had to go to hospital and the outcome was a transfer to the Northern Territory Administration (NTA) on light duties. This meant I had to move out of the DCA quarters and make my own accommodation arrangements. Familiar with Darwin by then I took a room in a boarding house half way between the CBD and the Administration property where I was sent to work as a yard man by the NTA. There were two of us to maintain the gardens and grounds.

The other bloke was part white and part aboriginal. The common terms were full blood, half-caste and quarter-caste. He showed me how to get a free snack from native passionfruit, berries and honey ants in the nearby Botanical Gardens and bush. I was saving as much money as I could to get back to Sydney. Having turned eighteen I was due to do National Service the following year. If I stayed in Darwin I would have had to train in Adelaide. Although I had distant relatives there it made more sense to go back home to train. Besides, Mum was now able to make ice cream.

For the benefit of young readers, ice cream was a treat back then. We couldn't go to a supermarket and buy a cheap big tub of ice cream like today. For a start there were no supermarkets let alone ice cream by the litre.

One Tuesday night I climbed up a big tree next to the *Star Cinema*. Only the rear seats had a roof, the rest were open air with a fence around the sides. The main feature was the 1951 film 'The Harlem Globetrotters' and it was Mission Night, that is to say the Mission Aborigines were brought into Darwin to see the picture. From my perch in the tree I had a good view. There is a part in the film where the basketball team is travelling from city to city by rail and the train appears to come right at the audience and run over them. That part resulted in the aboriginal audience screaming and taking off in all directions. I never did get to see the rest of that picture.

On the subject of cinemas, while I was in Darwin ABC Northern Territory radio news reported on an incident that happened in a small community down the Stuart Highway. Apparently once a week a film night was held in a local paddock. It was the practice to hang the screen from a tree with the projector mounted on the back of a truck and patrons sat on the ground. The picture showman was fined for not mowing the grass after one of the patrons was bitten by a snake.

Just before I left Darwin the wet season started. There were some really violent thunderstorms. On my way back to the boarding house late one afternoon, lightning struck a big gum tree as I was passing and split it from the fork down to the ground. I wasn't sorry to leave the Top End, it was too hot and humid for me.

I got a lift again as offsider on a semi down to Alice Springs and purchased a ticket on *The Ghan* to Port Pirie. I had to wait a few days for the train so it gave me a chance to do some sightseeing around The Alice. I also did some shopping, purchasing a pair of cotton gabardine trousers, a stockwhip and a pair of R.M. Williams boots. Down near The Gap I met a full blood aborigine who made me a hunting boomerang – not the fancy type sold to tourists.

The Central Australian boomerang, or karli, can be used to make a fire as well as being used as a knife, digging stick, ceremonial object or musical instrument. My one, which I still have, is made from the junction of a mulga root and trunk and is stained with red ochre which helps to preserve the wood. Utilising the natural curves of roots and branches was also the method used by early European boat builders for the ribs. Not all boomerangs are designed to return.

The trip in *The Ghan* was very slow even though the locomotive was diesel-electric. The problem was the track. In parts some passengers took to walking alongside the train and some blokes were throwing dead marines (empty beer bottles) out of the windows and using them for target practice. From Port Pirie I went by rail to Silverton, caught a taxi to the Broken Hill station and hopped on board the *Silver City Express* for Sydney. Along the way I saw lots of kangaroos and emus before it got dark. When I woke up the following morning the train was coming down the Blue Mountains. It arrived at Central Station soon after. I got off and thought I'd walk from Central to Town Hall station to stretch my legs.

Walking down the ramp near Belmore Park a bloke approached me and asked for a bob (shilling) to buy a cup of tea. Dressed as I was he took me for a bushie and a soft touch. I knew what he really wanted the money for but I gave it to him anyway. I was feeling good being back in my hometown. Going bush had been an enriching experience. At Town Hall station I caught an electric train to St. Leonards and walked up the Crowy.

12
NATIONAL SERVICE

Mum, Dad and Bob welcomed me home. However, four year-old John wanted to know who I was. He had forgotten me in my absence. It was coming up to Christmas and I was keen to get a job. While you were doing your National Service training your employer had a moral obligation to put aside the difference in your Nasho pay and I didn't want to miss out on that extra money. Government employers made up the difference but many private employers didn't so it made sense to get a government job.

At that time of the year it was difficult to find a permanent position but at the suggestion of Mum's brother Allan I applied for and got a job as a Station Assistant with the NSW Government Railways (NSWGR). Station Assistants were called porters back then. Mum's father had worked for the tramways and Uncle Allan worked for the NSWGR until he retired in the early 1990's.

At first I was assigned to look after the cloak room at St. James station below Hyde Park in the city. However, in the new year I worked as a relief up and down the North Shore line. It was shift work but the shifts were only seven and a quarter hours duration. It was a breeze after some of the jobs I'd had. Until I was called up I actually had a social life. When I got a crewcut haircut Dad hit the roof again.

On nights when I wasn't working my mate Kevin who lived opposite and I would either go to the pictures or to dance studios to learn ballroom dancing. These were pre-Rock 'n Roll days. We tried Phyllis Bates' in George Street across from the Queen Victoria Building, Jupp's above the Cremorne Orpheum and Bill Barnes' at Willoughby North. Once we got the hang of it, Phyllis Bates asked us to be dance teachers. We'd tried it for one night but decided we didn't care to be Fred Astaire and Gene Kelly. We had to have every dance whether we wanted to or not and got sore feet from being stomped on by some of the heavier ladies. The sweaty armpits of some of our partners was also a turn-off.

Things were more promising at the Willoughby North studio where I met Beverly. She lived in MacMahon Street around the corner from the dance studio. I walked her home that first night and we arranged to have a picnic at the Lane Cove National Park on the following Sunday. Beverly worked for a life assurance company in Martin Place as it was called then and said she would invite one of her work friends to accompany Kevin. Between then and when I was due for military service we went out regularly as a foursome.

While I was working in the cloak room at St. James station I read James Jones' 983-page epic novel 'From Here To Eternity'. Having played the bugle in the cadets and boxed a little I immediately identified with the Private Prewitt character. At about the same time the film was released and was jokingly referred to as 'From Here To Maternity'. As it happened I was made company bugler in the Nashos, helped along from my cadet days and the fact that I had also been having trumpet lessons in my spare time. My teacher was Marsh Goodwin who gave trumpet lessons in an upstairs room in King Street, Sydney.

On the appointed day I walked down to the 30th Battalion Drill Hall in Carlow Street, North Sydney and reported for duty. We all wore casual clothes and carried overnight bags containing our shaving and toiletry items. I was pleasantly surprised to meet up with some friends from high school days as well as familiar faces from Crowy. We eventually boarded buses and chatted on the trip out to the 13th National Service Training Battalion barracks. I had been to Ingleburn in the cadets and travelled around a large part of Australia so I felt at ease. However, some of the blokes who'd never been away from home before were very apprehensive.

When we arrived at Balikpapan Barracks we were lined up and the Regimental Sergeant Major (RSM) went into his act. Just for the record Balikpapan Barracks has since been renamed Bardia Barracks. Anyway, the RSM bawled us out and read the riot act to us after which we were kept on the hop continuously. We seemed to be either in neverending queues or lugging stuff about. We were issued with clothing, webbing, mess gear, linen, bedding and all the necessary items for army life, in addition to being sorted into companies, platoons and sections. We were also shown our huts, ablution and laundry blocks, mess huts, assembly areas, etc., etc. We no sooner got to sleep than we were woken up for roll call.

After three or four weeks army life seemed to get a little easier. We had been innoculated against various infectious diseases and with all the physical activities we were definitely much fitter bods. Shortly before I went into camp I got a toothache. With a considerable amount of Scottish blood in my veins I held off going to a dentist. I thought I'd wait and go to the army dentist for free. Big mistake!

It was a large molar and the dentist couldn't get it out. After trying for nearly an hour he gave me another needle and pulled out the tooth next to it so that he could get a better grip. When he finally got it out I looked like Popeye the Sailorman. His nurse kept giving him dirty looks as she fussed over me. It was the first time I'd had a tooth extracted and thought it was just the normal procedure. Everyone used to say they hated going to the dentist and one of Mum's girlfriends had died in her dentist's chair, so I expected the worst. Ignorance is bliss! Perhaps to console me the dentist arranged for our cook to give me soft foods for a week so I got to have goodies like ice cream and jelly to the envy of my fellow Nashos.

Days turned into weeks and weeks turned into months. I got mail from Beverly and saw her when I got leave. 'Once I Had A Secret Love' sung by Doris Day was on the Hit Parade at the time. One of our instructors told me that where my bed was in our hut was where Lew Hoad the tennis great had been two intakes earlier. As a consequence I was saddened in 1994 when it was announced on ABC News that he had died. On that subject, while I was doing National Service Pa died of cancer.

About half the blokes in our platoon were from the North Shore with the other half from the Newcastle area. I became quite friendly with one of the ex-NSTH school blokes. Tut and I had been in the same class one year. He had a relative in Los Angeles who was the top make-up artist at one of the major Hollywood studios with his name on the film credits. Tut had the same surname and was an avid student of the American Civil War and the Confederate States. He even had us both wearing our slouch hats like Johnny Reb's which often used to get us into trouble. I went along with it because Robert E. Lee Prewitt in 'From Here To Eternity' was a southern boy from the Kentucky Mountains. I still had my Walter Mitty moments while in the Nashos. Don't ever let anyone tell you that movies don't influence people. It's a pity Hollywood isn't setting a better example these days.

Apart from three particular incidents our platoon got through training without mishap. The first occurrence was when we were throwing hand grenades. After priming the grenades we moved forward two at a time to a dugout overlooking a creek where a regular army instructor was waiting. The Nasho with me was very nervous and dropped one of his grenades in the dugout after drawing the pin. Luckily the instructor was an old hand and tossed it over the sandbags in the nick of time. The second fright came when one of the blokes in our mortar team put a shell into the mortar upside down. It happened so quickly for a second we thought we'd be blown up. We sheepishly had to get up from where we'd dived to continue.

The last episode was when we went out for a mock battle with the whole battalion. We were due to move out at 2200 hours. When it started to rain cats and dogs about 2000 hours we rejoiced thinking it would be postponed. Hah! Wearing ponchos we marched all night in the pouring rain with our .303's and packs. By daylight we were at a place called the Woolwash on the Georges River east of Campbelltown. We had to cross over to the Military Reserve on the other side and scale a cliff. With all the rain that had fallen during the night the river was raging.

We formed a human chain and began crossing. With foresight our officers stationed the first troops to reach the other side, downstream at a bend in the river. It was just as well because a lot of bods got washed away due to exhaustion, our equipment and the sheer force of the water. We were lucky no one drowned.

During our time at Ingleburn some of us were chosen to participate in a display of physical fitness at the 1954 Military Tattoo at the Sydney Showground. After weeks of rehearsing we were transported by army trucks to the site of the Sydney Royal Agricultural Show where we were accommodated in tents for the duration of the Tattoo. Once again I was in familiar territory.

The year before I'd worked on the *Laff in the Dark* and the *Laughing Clowns* and camped there. As well as participating in the Tattoo we got to see it for free. If you've ever watched the Edinburgh Military Tattoo on television, or have been fortunate enough to see it live you'll have an idea of what goes on. Of course our Tattoo may not have been quite up to the same standard but, nevertheless, it was an impressive performance with motor cycle despatch riders going though rings of fire, precision drill, massed bands, mock battles and gun assembly competitions, etc.

We wore athletic singlets, khaki trousers and sandshoes and the highlight of our performance was falling over like dominoes. Formed up in concentric circles we had to fall face down which gave the impression of a huge flower opening up. For weeks we'd practised falling forward without reaching out with our hands and we got many a skinned nose in the process.

At the end of our basic training there was to be a *Passing Out Parade* at which friends and relatives could attend. One of the officers sent for me in my role as a bugler and told me I would be required to play 'Retreat' while the flag was lowered at the Parade. There were to be two buglers up on the dais with the brass and bigwigs. When I asked how many people would be there altogether he said, 'About two thousand or so'. I gulped and said, 'Maybe it would be better to ask one of the other Company buglers. I don't think I'm good enough'.

The officer looked me in the eye and said, 'If I tell you to eat sh_ _ you'll eat it. You can ask for pepper and salt to put on it, but you WILL eat it'. I was stuck and there was no way out. Between then and the big day I practised down by the creek at every opportunity. When I was in the cadets the bugle instructor who came to our school had told me to concentrate on hitting the right notes at the start and the finish. It didn't matter so much if you stuffed up in the middle, that would be overlooked or forgiven. As it turned out I got it right on the day. To make sure and for good luck I used my trumpet mouthpiece which was a #2 Kosicup. (A good name for a ladies bra!)

On the day we went home in November 1954 the morning was spent returning gear to the Q-store, cleaning out our huts and removing the identification flashes and patches from our shirts and tunics. Wearing our summer uniforms and carrying our kitbags we travelled by bus to Liverpool Railway Station where we were handed free train passes to our nominated stations. A small group of us chose to go to Wynyard in the city and have a farewell beer.

We arrived at Wynyard station just after lunch time and after checking our kitbags into the cloak room headed up the concourse to the Plaza Hotel Public Bar. On the way one of our blokes stopped at a newsagent and bought a midday-edition newspaper. On the front page was a photo of 3RAR (Royal Australian Regiment) who unbeknownst to us had marched through the city that morning. They had only recently returned from Korea and had been given a ticker-tape welcome home.

The Korean War had started in June 1950 when the Communist North invaded the South. Australia, as part of the United Nations force assisting the South Koreans, introduced conscription for all eighteen year-old males. There were also Communist insurgencies in Malaya and Vietnam and the threat of nuclear war between the West and USSR hung over the entire world.

The North Koreans were losing until Communist China came to their aid. An armistice was signed in July 1953 but because of the possibility of a flare-up, plus the other threats, conscription remained in force. One of our instructors had fought in Korea and had told us of his experiences so we knew a little of what it had been like. We were wearing the same uniform as 3RAR but without shoulder flashes to identify us until we joined our new units.

When we ordered our drinks some building workers in the bar called out to the barmaid, 'We'll pay for that, luv'.

I thought, 'This is alright, we do basic training and blokes buy you a beer'. Then the penny dropped. They thought we were 3RAR. One bloke sidled over to me and asked, 'What was it like up there mate?'

I took a sip of beer and said, 'Bloody cold mate'. It did get cold up at Ingleburn but nothing like the thirty degrees below freezing in the Korean mountains.

13
HAPPY DAYS

Over the next few months in my spare time I studied for and passed the exams to become a railway booking clerk. A position arose at Gordon station on the North Shore line and I duly took it up. At the same time I obtained a driving licence and purchased a 1938 Ford V8 with my back pay. I was a bit hasty in the choice of my first car. It was a real bomb and needed a lot of expensive repairs.

As it turned out a mate had bought a pre-war Standard 8 tourer which he was dissatisfied with and offered to swap his Standard 8 plus one hundred pounds cash for my Ford. I took him up on his offer even though the Standard 8 was also in poor condition.

With the money he gave me I got the Standard's engine rebored, replaced some parts, rubbed it down and gave it a new paint job. I also got a new canvas hood and mended the upholstery. I chose a lemon yellow colour for the bodywork and using my signwriting skills painted 'Genevieve' on both sides of the bonnet. The 1953 British film of that name about two couples and their vintage roadsters was one of my favourite films and still is.

I had a lot of fun in that little car even though it wasn't exactly what you'd call a hot rod. For example, when the 1955 Round-Australia Car Trial came up, using poster paint that could be easily removed, I plastered *Genevieve* with crazy, fake advertisements to make her look like an official entry and with my mate Kevin drove out to Parramatta where the Trial was to start.

Spotting our chance we joined the convoy as it travelled north up Pennant Hills Road then along the Pacific Highway. Our bogus official number, N° ½ was prominently painted on both sides and with the fake ad's such as 'Drink Ampol', 'Castrol Flakes For Breakfast', etc., we were shown on one of the newsreels.

As the weeks rolled by I saw less and less of Beverly. We still went out occasionally but I realised I didn't want to be involved in a serious relationship at that time. One of the perks working for the NSWGR was every so often employees were entitled to a free railpass within the State. I took my two weeks annual leave plus the Easter holidays and travelled by train up to Murwillumbah then caught a bus to Coolangatta. This time I was doing it in style. It was the first proper holiday I ever had without relatives.

Greenmount Guest House had opened in 1904 and during the 1950's and 60's was a magnet for holidaymakers. Coolangatta was known for its beach entertainment including the famous Hokey Pokey. There were also inter-guest house competitions on the beach and nightly outings to dances, roller skating, the cinema, etc.

I arrived at the guest house just on teatime. After leaving my luggage in the room I was to share with a bloke from Brisbane, I was escorted to the dining room and introduced to everyone at my allotted table by the Table Captain. Everything was highly organised. There were fifty guests – thirty girls and twenty boys. Good odds for the boys!

At one of the beach concerts I attended there was a comedy-impressionist act. I was sitting quite close to the stage and marvelled at his imitations of film stars and famous people. I'd been to the Sydney *Tivoli Theatre* and shows at the Sydney *Stadium* but had never seen anything like this bloke before. Then and there I resolved to learn how to do impressions. I met a girl from the Sydney suburb of Marrickville and we went out together a few times during the holiday.

There was one unusual contest between the guest houses called the *Choirmasters Competition*. It was actually a beer-drinking contest at a local pub. Drinkers were called choirboys and the winner got to wear a gob hat embroidered with the words 'Choir Master Coolangatta' which entitled him to free admission to various entertainment venues. One of our Greenmount boys won it while I was there. The reason for calling them choirboys was that if a girl told her parents she was going out with a choirboy they wouldn't worry.

After the holiday I saved up and purchased a second-hand wire recorder, the forerunner of tape recorders. Such equipment was expensive back then. Without the luxury of TV, video and DVD recorders I had to go to the pictures often and study the actors intensely, then practise with the wire recorder in front of a mirror when I could do so in private at home. Being on shift work helped in that respect. I was able to practise the voices and scripts I wrote while driving to and from Gordon as well. Whenever the wire snapped on the recorder as it rewound at speed it was the dickens of a job to untangle and rejoin it.

At Gordon Station I found I could do a good voice imitation of the Assistant Station Master (ASM). I worked in the booking office up on the bridge and sometimes after he came past on his way to the shops, I would ring down to the platform on the internal telephone and in the ASM's voice tell the unfortunate station assistant on duty to do some horrible task like clean out the men's toilet. It was one of the jobs station assistants had to do anyway.

In winter if I was on night shift Mum would put some stew, or curry, in a steamer for me to heat up. I would also toast a slice of bread on the radiator and top the meal up with a mug of hot tea. It was a comfortable life but I wasn't getting anywhere and I still had to complete my compulsory military training anyway, so I made the most of it.

There were quite a few regular Saturday night dances on the North Shore. Some mates and I would either go to the Police Boys Club Dance in Falcon Street, the Dispensary Hall Dance in Victoria Avenue, Chatswood or to one of the Catholic Youth

Organisation (CYO) Dances at North Sydney, Lane Cove, Turramurra and Waitara.

One night I took a home-made fake hand to the Lane Cove CYO Dance. The hand was easy to make. You filled a rubber glove with Plaster of Paris and let it set. It was then painted a flesh colour with red paint for the severed wrist. It was good timing because recently 'The Beast With Five Fingers', a 1946 horror film about a hand that strangled people, had been rescreened at the midnight 'Shiver, Shudder and Shake Show' at the Chatswood Hoyts' Esquire cinema.

After shaking hands with different blokes and leaving it temporarily in their grasp I went over to the kitchenette. As one of the girls came out through the batwing doors with a tray of tea and cakes I said to her, 'Would you like a hand?' and placed the fake hand on the tray. She let out a scream and dropped the tray. Tea and cakes went everywhere. I wasn't too popular after that prank.

Another night up at the Waitara CYO Dance Kevin and I arrived a bit late. There was a real glamour girl sitting down in front of the stage. Our mates told us she was the drummer's girlfriend and had refused all the blokes who had asked her for a dance. The drummer in the band was a really tough-looking bloke. They dared Kevin and I to ask her up. Kevin tried first and as predicted got knocked back. Then it was my turn. I knew that if she had refused all the other blokes she certainly wouldn't say 'Yes' to me. So I came up with an idea. 'I wuz de man wid a plan'.

Instead of asking her for a dance I asked if I could speak to her for a minute. She said, 'Yes', so I sat down next to her and told her that my mates had bet me that I couldn't get a dance with her. I then said, 'If you do I'll give you whatever I collect'. Well, blow me down if she didn't agree. We got up and as we danced I told her some of the funny things that had happened on my Gold Coast holiday and when she tossed her head back and laughed I noticed the drummer giving me dirty looks and my mates standing there with their mouths open. It couldn't have worked better if it had been staged.

After escorting her back to her seat I returned to my mates. One of them said, 'How come she got up with you, Parsons?' With a smug look I answered, 'Either you've got **it**, or you haven't got **it**'. Needless to say there was no money involved so there was nothing in it for Miss Glamour Girl and nothing for the drummer to worry about.

Occasionally Kevin and I would try some of the dances on the south side of the harbour. We tried one at Leichhardt, the Strollers at Marrickville (where I saw the girl from Greenmount), Vic's Cabaret at Strathfield and one that had a sprung dance floor in City Road near Sydney University. It was at Duffy's Tavern that I first saw and heard the Wild One, Johnny O'Keefe. His death at a relatively young age in 1978 was a great loss for the Australian entertainment industry and his many fans.

Some of the City cinemas changed programmes every couple of days and I would see at least one film a week. French had been a subject at high school and I used to enjoy French films at the Savoy Theatre from time to time. In the summer months if I was on night shift I would drive to either Balmoral or Manly, go for a swim then lie on the beach and read a novel. Carter Brown Private Eye stories were popular.

Early in 1955 I again fronted up at the 30th Battalion Drill Hall for further compulsory military service. However, this time there was a surprise in store for me – I was issued with a kilt and the bits and pieces that go with it. I should have realised. The 30th was the NSW Scottish Regiment. Although I had Scottish ancestors on my mother's side I regarded myself as a True Blue Aussie and preferred to dress like one. They didn't tell me how to wear the kilt so the first time I did I played it safe and wore underpants. I didn't know whether to wear both the sporran and the leather pouch or what.

When I asked one of the regular army blokes about underneath the kilt he replied, 'It's like this. On pay night the paymaster sits behind a desk. You march smartly over when called then stand at ease. There is a mirror set in the floor and if the paymaster looks down and sees you're wearing underpants you don't get paid. Does that answer your question?'

Through an officer I knew I got a transfer to the 17/18 Infantry Battalion in Stanley Street, Chatswood. That's where I met Billy when I joined the 17/18 Band. He lived at West Pymble. His father was regular army and had gone to the Queen's Coronation with the Australian contingent. Billy was a six-footer like myself only he was heavier. He resembled the film actor Lloyd Bridges.

Just after the terrible Hunter Valley floods in 1955 the 17/18 Battalion travelled to Singleton in army trucks for a two-week camp. I remember realising the extent of the flooding when I saw grass and debris hanging over telegraph pole crossbars and wires. When the convoy stopped briefly at Maitland a local told us a cow had been rescued from the branches of a tall tree.

One memorable night during that camp Billy and I went into Singleton on leave. At a local pub some other diggers dared us to 'Drink the shelf'. That's where you try to have one drink from every bottle on the shelves behind the bar. To put it mildly we got loaded then went to the local dance across the road. The hall was full of army types with only a few local girls and blokes.

Sitting opposite us were some NSW Scottish in their kilts. Billy crossed the dance floor and asked one of them for a dance. With the place full of bored, frustrated, fit young men it was suddenly on for young and old. When a hand grabbed my shoulder I spun around at the ready. It was Billy. He beckoned and mouthed, 'Follow me'. In the midst of the mélée we ducked out an exit door to a side passage. There was a bicycle leaning against the paling fence. Billy hopped on it and with him pedalling and me as passenger we wobbled down to the street and rode around in circles laughing our heads off before catching a bus back to camp.

I flaked out but Billy went off into the night to do some more stirring. The evening ended with him being placed on a charge. Mid-morning I was practising with the band and when I looked out the window of the band hut he was bared to the waist splitting firewood for our company kitchen. It had rained overnight and it was very hot and humid. When I next looked out he had disappeared. Shortly before lunch I went to our tent to get my bugle to play 'Cookhouse'. I played a cornet in the band. The tents held eight of us and Billy was bandaged-up sitting on his bed writing a letter to his girlfriend Annette.

'What happened to you?' I said imagining he'd injured himself with the axe.

'Nothing', he replied. He told me he had a hangover from the previous night and had gone up to the R.A.P. for a headache powder but it was unattended. There was a bundle of bandages on a table so he bandaged himself up then went over to the Orderly Room and told them he had to take it easy for a while. As it happened, one of Billy's uncles, a Real Estate Agent at Seaforth, was also a well-known radio actor under another name and read the commercials for a top brand of headache powder.

Just before we completed our part-time service prior to being placed on the reserve list in February 1957, Billy and I were invited to join a Commando Unit. We declined as it meant giving up our weekends and I had to work Saturdays anyway.

At the time I had started National Service in 1954, nuclear weapon testing became a matter of controversy when fallout from a test at Bikini Atoll was blown over three islands in the Marshall Group causing radiation sickness and burns to the Islanders and the crew of a Japanese fishing boat. By 1956 there had been over a hundred nuclear devices exploded by the USA, USSR and UK. Britain had been conducting tests in Australia since 1952 and there was widespread public concern about the effects of radiation fallout. There was even talk of our cow's milk being contaminated.

This was in addition to the threat of nuclear war between the USSR and the West plus a possible chain reaction. I mention this here purely to give younger readers a sense of the world situation at that point in time. Many National Servicemen were present at the British nuclear tests in Australia.

14
EXECUTIVE TRAINEE

Early in 1956 I noticed a used 1950 Holden for sale in the window of J.N. Caldwell's Showroom then in Alexander Street. It was in immaculate condition and I calculated that with *Genevieve* as a trade-in, my savings and a modest debt I could afford to buy it. However, as I was not yet classed as an adult, my father would have to go guarantor.

The legal age to vote, marry and sign contracts was twenty-one. It was unfair. I could be called on to defend my country but wasn't even entitled to vote. Dad flatly refused to go guarantor and I saw that as a lack of trust in me, or perhaps a touch of envy. At the time he had a nearly thirty year-old Canadian-built Durant he'd bought from a neighbour. The Durant cars were built by Wm. C. Durant who had founded General Motors but had been ousted in 1920.

When I'd started working full time the first things I purchased were clothes as my wardrobe consisted mainly of school uniforms. He didn't comment on the clothes. However, when I purchased one of the new portable radios to replace my crystal set he hit the roof. The American-style 'teen-age' market was only starting to be recognised in Australia. To Dad you were either a minor or, an adult. As a minor you did as you were told until you turned twenty-one.

I assured him I would never dream of letting him down with repayments. Reluctantly he signed as guarantor and I became the proud owner of a modern car. Most of the car owners I knew still had cars of pre-war vintage. *Genevieve* had been fun but I felt I'd passed that stage. I also felt I'd outgrown my job. Promotion was still by seniority in the NSWGR which seemed out-of-date to me. I thought it should be based on ability.

Woolworths' Executive Training Scheme had a good reputation and I was elated after being accepted. Trainees began in the Woolies' warehouse at Glebe then progressed through various office departments and finally the shops. You worked as a cleaner, storeman, counter jumper, section manager, assistant manager and hopefully manager. The training also involved working in a number of stores which were classified according to their size, etc. I worked briefly at the Liverpool Street, Oxford Street, Her Majestys and Wynyard branches before working locally at the Crows Nest store until the end of the year when I was transferred to Narrabeen.

Once I became a section manager I was given some difficult tasks to perform such as sacking a male employee and telling one of the sales girls she had B.O. (Body Odour). The other girls on her counter had complained to the Head Girl but the job of telling her fell to me. I was told by the Manager that it would be good experience for me and it was left to yours truly how to go about it.

She was a pretty girl and I told her as tactfully as I could, even suggesting she buy some deodorant and I would see to it that she was reimbursed from petty cash. If I had any thoughts of asking her out that put paid to that. She left shortly afterwards. I did go out with a couple of the girls and I found out that one of them was keen on me. She invited me to her birthday party which was held at her parents' home at Naremburn.

I got talking to her father about cars in the laundry where he had bottles of drink in the ice-filled wash tub. He said, 'I've been driving for twenty-five years and never had an accident'.

'That's pretty good', I said. Then he said, 'Hang on, I lie. Once up in the Blue Mountains I came around a bend on a narrow road and grazed an oncoming car but apart from that I've never had an accident'. He had a drink from his glass then, as an afterthought said, 'Hang on, there was another day ....' By the time he'd finished I reckoned he must have had an accident every time he got behind the wheel.

I was slowly maturing but every now and then would get up to childish pranks. One day a new line of water pistols came in for the toy section. They could squirt up to two hundred times without a refill. I filled one up, held it inside a paper bag and tore a corner off the bag to shoot through.

Whenever another male shop assistant or trainee was within range I'd squirt them. One time just as I pulled the trigger a middle-aged woman walked between me and the target. It caught her on the side of her head and I pretended to be putting a sales item in the bag. She held her hand out, looked up at the ceiling and said, 'I think the roof's leaking'.

Egg cartons had only just been introduced and a lot of customers were bringing their empty ones back for re-use, or expecting a refund. Consequently, we had a rubbish bag under the grocery section's counter full of empties. In one of my mischievous moments I filled an empty egg carton with ping-pong balls from the toy section and when the Head Girl came along, opened the lid and tipped the contents over her. She let out a loud scream thinking I'd gone mad showering her with eggs. The Manager raced out and led her to the rear of the shop to calm down. That was another trick I never played again.

Every Monday morning before the store opened there was a staff training talk usually by the Manager or Assistant Manager but sometimes by a trainee. Mostly they were dull and uninteresting affairs so when it came to my turn I thought of adding a bit of humour to liven things up. I worked out a script and enlisted the aid of Brian, one of the other trainees.

The first jobs for the counter staff each morning were placing change in the cash registers and cleaning and dusting their counters. The purpose of my talk was to persuade the younger girls not to chit-chat around the water buckets. Brian and I donned white smocks like the girls on the confectionery counter, with mop heads from the hardware section for long hair. We carried on talking and giggling in high-pitched voices about our night out with our boyfriends and made it a fun start to the week with a 'How Not To Do It' talk.

Since the holiday at Coolangatta I had maintained the interest in doing impressions of famous people, especially Hollywood actors and practised on the wire recorder whenever I could. I did a little act called 'The Hollywood Roving Reporter' where I pretended to interview the stars. To test reaction one day in the City on my way to Head Office I went up to the *Hotel Australia* and rang Reception from a public telephone in the foyer. Imitating James Stewart I told the girl I'd just arrived at Sydney Airport from Los Angeles and was checking to make sure my room was ready. It must have worked because I could see the desk staff running about in a flap from where I was standing. I hung up and left while the going was good.

Eventually at a Woolworths social evening held in a hall at Chatswood I tried out my 'Hollywood Roving Reporter' act for the first time and got a big thrill when it was well-received.

There were only about three thousand TV sets in New South Wales on Sunday 16 September 1956 when TCN Channel 9 began regular television broadcasting in Sydney. The next day brother John had his seventh birthday and two days later I turned twenty-one. Mum and Dad gave a party that night which was a rare event at 106. It was also the biggest party they ever had and the tiny house was packed with relatives, friends and neighbours. Dad was worried the flooring would give way and some of the residents in Burlington Street were concerned when a police patrol car pulled up outside our place. However, they were not to know it was my Uncle Frank who dropped in while on duty with a large gold-painted 21 key he'd made out of three-ply.

I was surprised when Beverly arrived as we'd not seen each other for some months. She gave me a beautiful inlaid chess set which I still treasure. I had played chess at high school and had the odd game some evenings with one of our neighbours. Finally the big moment came and after enduring numerous wisecracks I stood there humbly as everyone sang,

'Twenty-one today, twenty-one today,
He's got the key of the door ....'

EPILOGUE

Over fifty years on much has changed. Hardly anyone could have foreseen some of the things we take for granted today, such as personal computers, mobile phones and so forth. However, some things haven't entirely changed. Korea remains divided at the 38th parallel, Luna Park is still there alongside the Sydney Harbour Bridge and people still go to the cinema and listen to the radio. And whilst the residents of Burlington Street from the 1930's, 40's and 50's have either moved on or passed away, most of the original houses remain standing in one form or another.

It is said that history repeats itself but with a new twist each time. That appears to be the case at present with the Great Recession instead of the Great Depression.

When high debt levels and greed caused world stock markets to crash in 1929, what followed was bank failure, world trade taking a nosedive, businesses contracting or closing, a dramatic rise in the number of bankruptcies, high unemployment and government dithering. Through no fault of their own the majority of Australians were forced to endure years of hardship.

Once again, as in that earlier period, Australians are experiencing financial stress and unemployment - threatening or actual. Our troops are fighting in foreign lands and there is proliferation of nuclear weapons, plus the omnipresent bush fires, droughts, floods and shark attacks.

If that's not enough, today we have the added problems of terrorism, global warming, pollution, obesity, etc. On the plus-side mateship is alive and well and Australians remain as willing as ever to lend a helping hand when others are suffering. Fashion, architecture and technology may have changed but the ANZAC spirit remains constant.

On a personal note, having survived thus far I still dabble in art, drawing a regular comic strip for an Ex-service magazine as well as sketching and painting. To their credit, both of my brothers got through Sydney University while holding down full-time jobs, Bob doing Arts and Johnny doing Law.

Not far up the New England Highway north of Toowoomba where I now live is the town of Crows Nest. And just as on the lower North Shore in Sydney there are road signs indicating Crows Nest up ahead, so too there are similar road signs in Toowoomba. I get a warm feeling when I see those signs.

BIBLIOGRAPHY

Andrews, Graeme. The Ferries of Sydney, A.H. and A.W. Reed, Sydney, 1975.

Arndell, Ronald M. Pioneers of Portland Head, W.R. Smith and Paterson, Brisbane, 1976.

Murray, Robert. Go Well – One Hundred Years of Shell in Australia, Hargreen Publishing, Melbourne, 2001.

Ryan, John. Panel by Panel – An Illustrated History of Australian Comics, Cassell Australia Ltd., Sydney, 1979.

Warne, Catherine. Pictorial Memories Lower North Shore, Atrand Pty. Ltd., Crows Nest, 1990.